The Expat Almanac

The Frisky Geezer, LLC
Portland, Oregon, USA

Visit the Expat Almanac blog at www.expat-almanac.com

Printed in the United States of America

ISBN (print): 978-0-9887225-2-1

This book is also available in Kindle format
at www.amazon.com.

Contents

The Players

Louise Lague embarked on her first solo adventure at age three, after getting bored in her front yard. Her terrified parents kept her on a leash for thirteen years, then took her to Europe for the first time, which she found mindboggling and generally awesome. She can no longer count how many times she's been back, but never before for more than a month. A journalist, she wrote for Time Inc. magazines for twenty years. Her work has also appeared in *O, Self, Glamour, People*, and the *New York Times* travel section.

Tom Lichty dabbled in the wine exporting business for years, not to make money (he didn't), but to travel (he did), and discovered that travel is like a fine pinot noir: adventurous, savory, and somewhat addictive. He is retired as a graphic-design consultant and university lecturer. Over half a million copies of his books have been sold. Interspersed with legitimate employment, he has been a pilot, a radio announcer, a tugboat operator, and a newspaper publisher.

Contrary to the photo on the cover, we are not traveling in a van. We don't own anything that resembles a van or a car. Nomadic lifestyles and automotive ownership are mutually exclusive, far as we can tell.

Introduction

Louise and I are well into our second fifty years. Our kids have fled the nest and the retirement accounts are in place. We can still walk to the corner, we don't drool, and although we never seem to remember all of our passwords, we do remember birthdays and Christmas, which seems to be enough.

But retire? You mean golf and bingo and a condo in Florida? That kind of retire? That's not us. Instead we abandoned comfort and security, sold almost everything we owned, packed one bag each, and embarked on an adventure that lasted a year.

This book is about that adventure.

— *Tom Lichty*

Chapter 1: The Nexus

What a moment in life!

That's the kind of thing we said when our first child was born, or when we ate our first bite of Duck a l'Orange, or ~~when we did our first hit of acid.~~ (Forget I said that. I admit to misbehaving a bit, and listening to Hendrix, and living ten miles from Ken Kesey's farm, but acid? No. Not acid. Not that I can recall…)

But I digress. I'm talking about now! This moment in life.

Let's give a look at it. As I said in the introduction, Louise and I are in our second fifty years. One would like to think that during those fifty-plus years, we've acquired a survival kit for life: tolerance, enlightenment, humility, and wisdom. Lots of wisdom. We're also at that life's moment where the nest is empty, our fiscal house is in order, and we have the time to experience a variety of adventures. Or some combination thereof.

Isn't that grand? That's what I mean by this moment in life. It's an avalanche of blessings, abetted by experience, enabled by aging. It's all some kind of kismet.

Now there's a word: *kismet*. In some Serbo-Croation dialects, they define kismet as "luck." Are we lucky to be where we are in life? Yes, but it's not just luck. Life woulda snuffed us fifteen years ago if we hadn't deliberately practiced humility, tolerance, fiscal responsibility, and a willingness to accept medical advances. It's not all luck, but this isn't a Serbo-Croation dialect, either. As a descriptor for our fortuitous moment in life, kismet is a pretty good word, and if there was a kismet index, Louise and I would be near the top.

In graphical form, kismet might appear as it does on the next page:

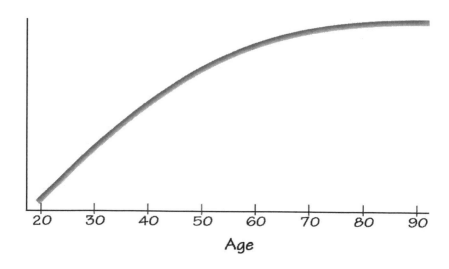

Age

A lovely, predictable, upward slope of kismet, forever reaching toward nirvana, unerringly maturing with age. What a moment in life!

But enough of this feel-good, pat-ourselves-on-the back kismet stuff. We all know there's a dark side, and the dark side to aging is health. Back when we were in our invincible twenties, health was no more significant to us than, say, Serbo-Croatian dialects. But now, in our second fifty years, health is the elephant in the room. Between the two of us, Louise and I have survived strokes, heart attacks, hip replacements, corneal implants and some other things that we prefer not to talk about. We've emerged from traumatic injuries grateful, enlightened, and more than a little circumspect. A feeling of "I've gotta live for the moment" pervades. Health—or the lack of it—is gonna get us, but until it does, well, there's the moment.

Which brings us to our second graph. Plotted over time, health might look like the one on the next page:

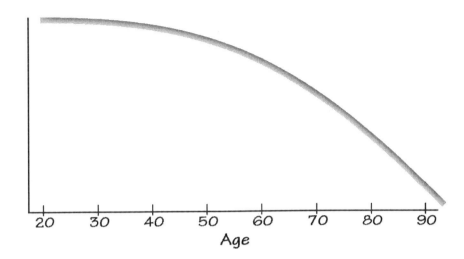

Not a pleasant sight, but inevitable. We'll not linger here. Instead, a look at the two graphs together:

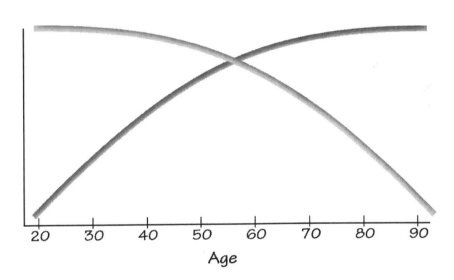

And there it is: the nexus. Right there where the two lines cross — and a few years on either side — that's where we are. We have yet to achieve the nirvana of kismet, but we're not dead either. This is why we decided to travel until the soles of our shoes wear through.

This nexus is a fleeting moment. It hasn't presented itself in our lives before and it won't again. Wasting it is like wasting a honeymoon, or a rainbow, or the spontaneous urge to dance. Recognizing the nexus is the beginning; affirming it is the process; exploiting it is the reward.

Chapter 2: The Plan

With appreciation of the Nexus upon us, we considered our options. The golf-and-bingo option was out. The word "adventure" crept into our discussion and, like a fragrant aroma, lingered. Adventure, after all, is the best way to keep from growing old. We both equate travel with adventure, so travel it was going to be. A discussion ensued.

Since I'm a horrible student of languages but have always wanted to learn Spanish, I suggested we travel to Spanish-speaking countries where I could immerse in a sea of trilled r's and n's with tildes. Immersion, however, requires ... well ... immersion, and that eliminates short stays. Months, if not years, would be required (I'm a slow learner), and to be able to afford that, we would have to move out of our apartment, sell everything, and become vagabonds. We preferred the word *expats*.

A decision like this is not to be taken lightly. Homelessness means there's no going back. We decided on a trial run. Louise is fluent in French and wanted to exercise her skills. Thus, April of 2012 found us in the lovely coastal village of Collioure, France. We lived there for a month and returned confident in our adaptability and emboldened by our enthusiasm. Our apartment lease was to expire March 31, 2013. We wouldn't renew.

While we were in Collioure we explored the countryside. Nearby we discovered Girona, Spain. Spain was much less expensive than France, Girona was just big enough to entertain us, yet small enough to feel at home in—and, being Spanish, it satisfied the immersion requirement (more about that later).

And so a decision was made. We would begin by living in Spain. Meanwhile, what about the mountains of stuff we collected over the years? What about the car? What about visas? What about health care? What about banking? What about mail? What about...?

We had a year to get ready.

Chapter 3: Anticipation

This book was inspired by a blog that we started a few days after we decided to embark on our journey. We announced our intentions in the first post, then emailed a hundred friends and associates, asking them to tune in. We wrote the blog not only because we're both addicted to writing (Louise was an editor at Time, Inc. for twenty years; I was a newspaper publisher for twelve), but also because we wanted to sabotage any escape to our plan. There's nothing like telling a couple dozen fellow journalists (and good friends, and our children) of our outrageous folly to guarantee our commitment.

The blog is at http://expat-almanac.com. There are pictures.

Below, a post I wrote on Tuesday, September 12, 2012, six months before our planned departure.

—§—

Remember that Carly Simon song, "Anticipation"? It was cleverly used in a Heinz ketchup commercial in the late 1970s. It has been running through my head lately.

> We...
> Can never know about the days to come,
> But...
> We think about them anyway.

We've all been reminded that tomorrow may never come, to live in the moment. Louise and I try to do that. We really do. But our lives are hurtling toward a tectonic shift. In six months we will have no home, few belongings, and only fading memories of stability, predictability, and grace.

Commensurately, we refine our lists, investigate places to live, and correspond with ex-pats around the world. To a degree, these activities—dreams and illusions, perhaps—are our moment. Our respiration. Our *vivendi causa*.

We went to a movie last night. We spent a couple of days at the coast last week. We went out for breakfast Sunday morning. These are all living in the moment; but in the evening, when we pour a drink and sit on the balcony, we talk about—not the moment, but the morrow. If it's not *the* moment, at least it's *our* moment.

We may never know about the days to come. But we think about them anyway.

Chapter 4: The Spanish Visa

Meanwhile, on with the story. With Girona as a destination, the next step was to investigate the Spanish Visa situation. Here's my blog entry for June 5, 2012:

—§—

If we intend to stay in Spain for more than ninety days, we'll need visas. My investigation began today with a visit to The Spanish Ministry of Foreign Affairs and Cooperation website which, among other things, is charged with "promoting Spain's economic, cultural and scientific relations."

These are the people who will issue our visas and they're interested in promoting a cultural (and economic) relationship with us. Cooperation! It's right there in the title.

I navigate to the visa page and read the first paragraph:

The procedures and conditions for issuing these visas are set out in Organic Law 4/2000...

Organic Law? Thank God for Google. Turns out organic laws are *really important* laws, residing just below the Spanish Constitution. The mind reels with thoughts of disobeying laws like that.

The visa page continues:

The visa application must be made in person in the Diplomatic Mission or Spanish Consular Office in the country in which the applicant legally resides.

Oh-oh. They say "in person." A few more clicks and I discover the nearest consular office — in San Francisco.

There's more:

If the visa application is successful, the visa must be collected from the Diplomatic Mission or Consular Office in which the application was submitted within a period of one month from the notification date.... The visa must be collected in person...

Two trips to San Francisco? For each of us? A quick online check on airfares and some rudimentary math points to a total transportation cost of about $1000, and that doesn't include getting around in the city or lodging. (Do you think we're going down there and back in one day? And dealing with Spanish bureaucracy while we're there?)

As for the documents required, here's a list:

- *valid passport with at least two blank pages*
- *confirmation letter from your health insurance stating coverage & one copy*
- *hotel booking in Spain & one copy*
- *closed round-trip or tour ticket*
- *current bank statement & one copy*

This doesn't look good. We have no idea where we're going after we leave Spain, so there will be no round-trip tickets. And wouldn't it be a bit premature to book an apartment before seeing if we can get visas?

Maybe the Americans can help. I visit the Department of State website and find this:

U.S. citizens who wish to stay in Spain for longer than three months...will also need to supply local authorities with an official criminal records check from their state of residence or from the Federal Bureau of Investigation's Criminal Justice Information Services office. Both types of documents must be apostilled by the state authority for state criminal records and by the Department of State for the FBI records.

Criminal records? Apostilled? *The FBI?!!*

I need a drink. And a dictionary.

Chapter 5: A Place to Glamp

Louise is our travel agent. She loves to troll online for lodging and travel, and she's VERY good at it. We have traveled the world, on trains, buses, and airplanes; we have stayed in glamorous lodgings (almost all, by the way, secured for less rent than our apartment in Portland); and we have dined in restaurants worthy of Michelin stars (but at prices that border on larceny).

Thus, it fell to Louise to find a home for us in Girona. She did, with her usual applause-worthy success. Our rental was for 89 days, just shy of the 90-day no-visa limit. Below, her account from June 7, 2012:

— § —

Found: A Place to Glamp!

Which is, of course, glamorous camping, and a bit of a joke in this case. Today, if our nerve stays with us, we will send the deposit on our chosen rental in downtown Girona, Spain.

As a lover of old towns everywhere, I had in mind an ancient building with exposed brick walls, low beamed ceilings, perhaps a turret with a ghost.

Charm is great, but we have learned that apartments built before plumbing and electricity are not likely to have those twin necessities: WiFi and a dishwasher. They often have a paucity of electrical outlets. (Blogging from a Starbucks in Barcelona, I noted not a single outlet in the wall. Why? The ceiling, an elaborate ancient waffle and bas-relief gilded event, could not be disturbed by installing wires. I quite agree, but my battery was on strike.)

So when I came across a modern penthouse apartment online, I balked at its spiraly rug thing, but knew that probably it would all work. There is WiFi, there is air-conditioning, there is a dishwasher and a clothes washer. And an elevator. (YES!!!!!) Best of all, there are windows on three sides. Tom will do his online work at a desk in a little glass box that juts onto the deck. I will cook paella in a real kitchen with a wall-size view of the cathedral atop the Old Town.

We will soak in our hot tub on the deck and entertain at the outdoor table for four. We will lift glasses of cava and toast all our friends new and old, and we will retire into bed in a cozy nook.

Writing this reminded me that all real estate is emotional. One doesn't choose a home using just a checklist. We all see ourselves using that potential space to create a life we want. Will it happen just like that? Maybe, maybe not. We're taking a chance on it. When we adventure, we must be ready for all sorts of surprises. If we weren't, we'd just stay home.

Chapter 6: Home is Where the Head Is

With a year to think about our upcoming adventure, there was plenty of time for philosophical musings. Here's mine from September 6, 2012:

— § —

We talked this morning about the concept of "home." If we're to become serial expats, living here and there for three or six months at a time, will we feel homesickness? And if we feel it, for what home will we feel sick?

We decided that it's more than an address. We'll have to have an address for the banks and healthcare people. We'll probably use my daughter's address for that. But that's not home.

Is it the place where we grew up? I grew up in Eugene (OR); Louise grew up in West Warwick (RI). They're familiar places. Our schools are there. But neither one of us has lived in those places for decades and we don't miss them. They're not home.

Is it family? "Home is where the family is." That works for millions of people worldwide, but probably least for people in the US. We tend to go to where the jobs are, and ours is a big country. Some of us go to places that appeal to us and then find a job. Regardless, we move. Frequently. The Bureau of Labor Statistics of the U.S. Department of Labor says that the median number of years that wage and salary workers had been with their current employer was 4.0 years in January 2006, unchanged from 2004. So, for North Americans, one might suppose that home is where the job is — not where the heart is, nor where the family is. At the moment, Louise and I feel fortunate that all of our children are at least on the US West Coast, within nice train rides of each other.

Objectively speaking, a home is shelter. It keeps you dry. It keeps you warm. It offers places for sleeping, social interaction, food preparation (and consumption), and — this may be the most critical of all — water. (Could you live in a home without water?) To that list, we add Internet. But that's just us. Is that enough? Is that home?

I've decided — and I haven't consulted with Louise on this — that a home is simply a place where I want to be. Not just the abode, but the community and the environment with which it's associated. That allows for change: I want to be in Girona next spring, but not so much next summer. I want to be on the Mexican coast in the winter, but not so much during the hurricane/rainy/humid season in July and August.

In the end, home is a subjective issue. It differs from one person and one time to another. For me, home is where I'm stimulated, where I'm sustained, where I'm comfortable, happy, fed, and bathed — all transient values. They change with the season, with my stage of life, with my sense of adventure, and with my companion's caprice. Home is where I am. Today. Now.

Whew! I feel so much better for having written that. Now I know why becoming a serial expat is so attractive. And why, perhaps someday, I'll find something else to be equally attractive. Home is not in Girona, or Portland, or Mexico. Home isn't where the job is or even where the heart is: home is where the head is.

Chapter 7: Bag and Baggage

I don't have a monopoly on philosophical musings, although Louise's tend to lean more toward the practical. Here's her post from September 7, 2012, six months before departure:

—§—

While Tom writes rhapsodic thoughts about the true meaning of home, I am pondering luggage. He is a poet; I am a Capricorn.

You already know that classic luggage comes in three sizes:
- small (20-21 inches, carry-on size)
- medium (24-26 inches, needs to be checked)
- and humongo (30 inches, needs to be rolled).

So what to bring for a possible whole year away? Faced with the sheer length of the trip, Tom's idea was to each bring two big 30-inch suitcases. That ought to do it, right? After all, the first three months are all in one spot: Girona.

Then I got to envisioning how we travel. We are never trailed by an army of porters with carts. We will be bumping these bags up and down staircases in train stations and quaint hotels, in and out of cabs. We will be stuffing them into tiny rental cars, and perhaps into a tiny ship's cabin.

Though packing less is an odd position for me to take, given how many shoes I will need, schlepping large bags around is a fate that, for me, is worse than going barefoot. And so I suggested one big bag each. Tom got out his tape measure and ran it all around our two big bags and declared them both within the airline's legal limits. And internationally, the first bag flies free, so, wow, what a savings. He thought he could manage.

Meanwhile, I packed up my 25-inch hardside Delsey, superlight and cute, to go East for a week. And with my necessary stuff inside, it weighed 47 pounds, very close to the international limit of 50. Gosh, if that's what the medium weighs, how much will the large weigh? I shudder.

And so, I craftily mentioned the possibility of downsizing once again.

"What?" he said. "You want me to do it all in a backpack?"

"No. How about one medium suitcase each?"

So here's what's happening. We've each made a packing list already, and one of these days we're going to actually rehearse the packing to see if we can get everything on the list into 25 inches and what it will weigh. We'll let you know. Maybe we can wheedle it all down to a small rollerbag, or maybe even a tote bag! What a challenge!

Chapter 8: Summer, Fall, Winter

Louise booked our Girona apartment for April, May, and June of 2013. This she accomplished in June of 2012. Months passed while we contemplated what was to come. We researched Spain and Girona, trains and ferries, bags and baggage. We become Trip Advisor devotees. We drew up packing lists and things to do.

Then, in early October, Louise the travel agent booked another apartment. Here's her entry from October 1st, 2012:

—§—

We're popping open the champagne tonight because we reserved another apartment today—this one in Chania, on Crete, in Greece, for the month of July, 2013. No, we've never been there.

How did we come to commit to yet another town we'd never heard of? First, we thought Greece needed our humble help. Then we thought that its miles of shoreline might provide an actual hot summer-beachy experience, which one does not get in Oregon even if you sit on the beach all year.

We get a lot of advice from online travel guides, local chambers of commerce, and tripadvisor.com (where Tom asks such beautifully crafted questions that he gets slews of answers). We check the historical averages of the weather, we read actual paper guidebooks (while huddled in Powell's City of Books), and we peruse expat sites.

We take that advice under consideration and cherish most of it—but not all. We ignored Rick Steves' advice to center ourselves in Rethymnon (which is also on the north shore of Crete). We chose Chania because it is, we understand, the most beautiful and the oldest. It appears to have been inhabited since the Neolithic era— some 12,000 years! It has medieval castles, quaint Fourteenth Century townhouses, and narrow cobblestone streets. We require this.

We ignored someone's advice that we should spend only three days in Chania— that we would perish of boredom if we stayed longer than that. Chania is older than dirt. We can probably deal with a month.

We ignored advice to rent slightly outside of town. We like the whole foreign-city scene: the sound of the last revelers at night and the trash cans clanging at dawn, the scent of roasting lamb, the thick Greek coffee at the Internet cafe. The ambiance of a city — especially one of the oldest cities on the planet — tickles our adventuring spirit.

Finding an apartment was the last step. We needed good WiFi, good air conditioning (this will be summer in Greece, after all), a nearby beach, and at least a scrap of kitchen. And the apartment has to be big enough that we don't bump into the furniture or each other every time we turn around.

We read all the reviews and everything we can find about every candidate apartment. We look at the map and the satellite view. We pull up images on the Internet. We correspond with owners and ask stupid questions. (Though I have not yet figured out how to phrase the question: "But is your WiFi any good?")

After a few weeks, we zeroed in on the Anastasia Apartments, and corresponded with a lovely lady named Katerina Nikoloudaki. Tom likes the looks of the spiral staircase. I had to make sure that the bed and the bathroom were on the same floor. Now the deposit is on its way.

−§−

We took a couple of weeks off after that and flew down to Puerto Vallarta, a likely candidate for our winter of 2013-14. We'd visited PV (as it's called) before. We knew we loved it. It's on the Pacific coast of Mexico and relatively close to our children. But if we were going to live there for six months, we wanted to see our place before booking it.

By the end of October, I had posted another entry in the blog:

−§−

We have returned from Puerto Vallarta, Mexico. It was hot and muggy, but the alternative was rain in Portland. In Portland when it rains, there's no escaping the wet. In Puerto Vallarta when it gets hot, there's always the Pacific. And the margaritas...

In spite of an army of timeshare salesmen who tried to convince us otherwise, we fell in love with PV. We love the people. We love the weather. We love the ocean. We love the place so much that we booked an apartment for six months in a neighborhood called Los Tules, starting October 1, 2013.

Inside the apartment, a spiral staircase leads to a soaking tub in the upstairs bedroom. Outside, a wide beach leads to the Pacific. There are two air conditioning units, two baths, two swimming pools, and three beds. It's Paradise.

Just like Puerto Vallarta itself.

Chapter 9: A Year of Homes

We were on a roll. We had booked apartments for an entire year, save for August of 2013. By November 5 of 2012, we had filled the gap. Here's my post:

— § —

It was 2002, I believe. Ten years ago. Traveling alone in Italy with five days to spare, I pointed the rental car north and discovered, unwittingly, Lake Como. George Clooney hadn't purchased Villa Oleandra yet (that came a few months later). They say the lake changed after Clooney's arrival. I hope it hasn't changed much, because we've just rented an August apartment there.

The lake is in the far north of Italy, surrounded by the Alps, quaint villas, and ancient *comunes* (towns), but to my eyes the town of Bellagio is the fairest of all. Lake Como is the shape of an inverted "Y," and Bellagio is at the intersection, where the mountain views abound.

Our lodging is a garden apartment (which is good — we'll need that garden in August) with a fireplace (which we won't need) and a full kitchen.

With the booking in Bellagio, our year is complete:

- Girona, Spain — April through June, 2013
- Chania, Greece — July, 2013
- Bellagio, Italy — August, 2013
- USA (visiting children) — September, 2013
- Puerto Vallarta, Mexico — October, 2013 through March, 2014.

The adventure begins in April. It feels as if we're five years old on the night before Christmas. The waiting is excruciating. Exquisite, but excruciating.

— § —

We had four months to go.

Chapter 10: It's the Little Things That Hurt

By mid-November we were facing the "sell everything" part of becoming expats. It's easy enough to say, but like climbing a mountain, the actual path of the doing is littered with obstacles and riddled with forks. In her November 6, 2012 post, Louise described one:

—§—

I was chatting with my son Ted about our adventure, and admitted I was a little scared. (Don't worry—I have run all the cognitive-therapy questions and I know intellectually that leaving home is no scarier than staying home. But I will allow myself to be scared anyway, because it's a normal reaction to a big forthcoming change.)

He said, pithily, "Seems like the scariest part would be packing up." *Bingo!* Yes, indeedy. Reshaping the possessions pile. Deciding between keep/toss/store/pack. Ridding oneself of bits of the past. The unhappy bits are already gone, as I have moved five times in the last ten years. But some of the happy bits need to go, too.

Focusing off the really big changes, I am obsessing about… accessories. I am attached to my scarves, bracelets, shoes, bags, necklaces, shawls, earrings, and watches. When I was unable to find affordable jewelry that was big enough for me, I started to make my own. Imagine how much more attached I am to the things I've made! And that spurred this enormous bead collection…things waiting to be made.

And some were gifts—from my children, my beloved Tom, best friends and relatives now far away or passed on. Many are souvenirs of travels around the world: when others buy teeshirts, I buy earrings or scarves. Silver from Mexico, gold from Turkey, silk from Spain, scarves from France, a fur hat from Canada, a wool shawl from Germany. They are small and packable, and up to now I haven't had to lose any.

Will anybody else get this if I say too good for Goodwill? Lots of my stuff is headed there, no problem. But there are some things that I want to sell personally. I want to watch them go, and see who they're going to, and hear someone say "You made this? I love it!" I guess that means I want to be validated as my still-loved accessories go away.

Of course the flip side of watching them sell is the way certain people without taste will fling some of this stuff aside.

So how do I do this? Do I do it piece by piece on eBay? Do I set up a table in the apartment and put an ad on Craig's List? Do I want people stomping around my apartment? Do I invite only people I know? Do I give the proceeds to charity? Do I seek a neutral event space? Does it have to be this hard?

I keep telling myself that there is nothing to fear. I am not becoming homeless; I am becoming a citizen of the world. My children are grown up and they don't need me hovering around. I love hovering around them but I'll still be able to do that whenever I want; it's just a longer, more expensive flight. So nothing to fret about, really. But I will anyway. Better to worry about earrings.

Chapter 11: I Feel Like a Red Balloon

The year of departure—2013—arrives, and by the end of January we're immersed in the throes of anticipation and preparation. There's not enough time/there's too much time before we walk out of our apartment, our city, our state, our country, our lives as we've known them.

January 30, 2013. Louise is feeling the pressure:

—§—

Sixty days to liftoff!

Yes, it's exciting, but I'll admit I have had more nightmares about liquidation than I have had happy dreams about Europe. In my head, the issues involved in getting rid of stuff looked like…you know when your earbuds get all tangled up in your pocket and they won't unknot?…like that.

Throw a tag sale? Donate? Rent trucks? Put a dumpster outside the apartment? And where to sleep when the bed goes to storage? How to *get* to storage after we sell the car?

I have accused my adorable Tom of being parsimonious in the past, but on this occasion, he has been saying: "Professionally-run estate sale." Really? Would any estate sale maven worth her salt want a batch of Ikea black tables in different shapes and a dozen lamps that came from Goodwill to begin with?

It turns out that Robin Caton of Found Stuff Estate Sales wants to sell it. She wants to sell our furniture, computers, my costume jewelry, my Chinese jackets—even the champagne corks. "Don't even bother to throw out the food," she says. "We'll sell that, too." Even the buckets of protein powder I bought in a crazy fit of faux fitness? "Even that."

Here's the drill: We put the family antiques in storage. We pack our bags for Europe. We move to a friend's house on March 19th. Robin moves in to our apartment with tables, tags, signs, and hefty mover folk. On March 23rd and 24th, there is a tag sale. We will try not to hang around outside. Seventy-two hours later we get a check. Not a big one, but that's not the point. The check goes in the bank, and the next day we fly.

We hired Robin half an hour after she walked through our door. Suddenly an enormous weight was lifted from our hunched shoulders. No kidding. I feel like I've turned into that red balloon in the movie, floating over Paris. Time is freed up to throw dinner parties, say our good-byes, hug the children, pack and repack, go to all the Oscar-nominated flicks, and of course, dream about Europe. At last.

Chapter 12: The Home Stretch

Having contracted for the tag sale, an onerous burden was lifted from our minds. Robin will eliminate all our stuff! All we have to do is box up things we can't part with, put them in storage, and leave the rest for the sale. The apartment will emerge empty and "broom clean," and — if we're lucky — we'll have a few dollars in the bank as well.

That part about boxing up became Louise's interest in this post, from February 18, 2013:

— § —

At last I have something in common with the great novelist Ann Beattie: an insatiable need for free boxes. She too is moving, and writes in the February 17th New York Times: "Boxes are much on the itinerant person's mind. I brood about lost boxes, boxes I received via UPS — those Zappos boots! — that I stupidly took to the recycling center."

During the last nine months or so, none of our boxes have made it to the recycling center. We will need them all for storing the stuff we're not selling or bringing along. Several stacks worth of free boxes — previously used — have been growing around the apartment. For a while, we couldn't even find the office light switch.

The collection got a huge boost when an eyelash salon moved to our building. Kimmi ("Miss Knockout") gave us boxes that had held furniture, supplies, rugs — even appliances. What a rich collection!

Christmas was quite a boon to the box collection, and of course, expat preparation has necessitated a flurry of online shopping. Barely a day goes by that Tom or I don't push the Amazon One-Click button to bring in a money belt, the perfect camera, an inflatable travel pillow, comfy shoes, quick-dry underwear — always ordered one item at a time. We get more boxes that way. None have been abandoned.

We started to pack a week ago. We are no longer flinging the empty boxes from room to room in order to find the light switch or the washing machine. Flinging is no longer an option, as empty boxes are turning into full ones. We just hope we won't have to — *gulp!* — buy any.

Chapter 13: Contraband

Robin pulled off the tag sale without a hitch. We returned to the apartment the day after and the place was broom clean, as promised. A couple of hours later and it was in good enough shape to qualify for a full refund of our deposit. We left the keys on the counter and walked out the door for the last time.

Were we frightened? Did we question our decision? Did our heads need to be examined? Yes, yes, *yes!* But everything was behind us now — and everything was ahead. The only thing left to do was count our cash. Here's my entry from March 27, 2013:

– § –

Robin paid in cash. Wads of bills and pocket change. All told: $1,969.47. I carried it to the bank — surreptitiously looking around me as I walked — and dumped it on an unsuspecting teller as if it was contraband. Which in a way, is what it was.

I'm talking about the proceeds from our estate sale. I suppose I could be penurious and ask, "Is that all we're worth?" But to tell the truth, the money really does seem like contraband. When we think of all the Craig's List ads (and phone calls, and deliveries), and all the trips to donation centers that we would've had to endure, the service that Robin provided would have been a bargain if she had simply emptied our apartment for free.

(At Robin's insistence, we left food on the shelves — open jars of peanut butter! — toiletries in the bathroom, even socks in drawers. At estate sales, people actually buy half-full bottles of shampoo. We removed what little we intended to store, and left everything else *in situ*.)

So here we are. Three days from departure. Homeless, with practically nothing to call our own. Will we miss our friends, our families, our favorite pub up the street? Yes! But will we miss all that stuff on the shelves and in the drawers? Are you kidding? This is freedom!

Chapter 14: Jet Lag

And so it was that on April 1st, 2013 — yes, April Fool's Day, but in 2013 it was also Easter Sunday and one sort of mollified the other — we found ourselves on a Condor Airlines flight (Condor is a German subsidiary of Lufthansa, and highly recommended) destined for Barcelona. It's a long flight from Portland to Barcelona, and there's a nine-hour time difference as well. In other words, jet lag was a factor. Here's my entry from April 4, 2013:

— § —

At ricksteves.com, Louise's favorite travel guide says, "On arrival, stay awake until an early local bedtime." Yeah, but Rick isn't turning 70 in thirteen months.

Jet lag. It gets worse every time I travel, in spite of elaborate preparations. For this trip I purchased a butt pillow, and that helped. (I lament having no butt — women tell me I'll never qualify as a hunk without it — and feel exquisite pain after an hour of sitting.) I researched inflatable neck pillows until I found The Perfect One (davidsbeenhere.com). I avoided alcohol, even though Condor offered it for free. I even surreptitiously swallowed half a Seroquel on the plane while I thought no one was looking. Nonetheless, when we checked into our Barcelona hotel at 1:00 PM last Sunday, I was asleep by 1:10.

So much for Rick Steves.

But wait! It doesn't make any difference! In Spain, everything except the bars shuts down around 2:00 PM. No groceries. No shoe shopping (a moment of pity for Louise). No banking or dentistry or museums. People just flee the city and don't return until 5:00, when everything reopens — and stays open until nine or so in the evening.

Thus, without even a dollop of compromise, Louise and I sleep four hours at night, visit the park or the museum or the bank in the morning, nap until four or five, then carouse in the evening — often until past midnight. No jet lag!

Spain is such a civilized place…

Chapter 15: When Catalonia Takes Over the World

Attentive readers may recall that a primary factor in determining not only our stay in Spain, but in determining this entire adventure was Tom Learns Spanish By Immersion. How could I avoid it? Live in Spain (and, in the winter, Mexico) and become fluent. Bilinguality guaranteed!

There was a significant flaw. Although Girona is in Spain, it's in a part of Spain called Catalonia. The politics were such that Catalonia would have liked nothing better than to secede from Spain. Catalan flags hung from every building, and—importantly—people spoke the Catalan language. Spanish? Hardly a hint.

Here's Louise's entry from April 9, 2013:

−§−

Nothing could have prepared me for Catalan. Well, maybe my sixty years of French study and forty years of Spanish study and those two miserable years of Latin. But the Catalan independence movement around here has become so fierce that the signs and menus are no longer bilingual in Catalan and Castilian Spanish, as they were just last year. It's all Catalan, all the time.

Derived from ancient rustic Latin spoken by Roman soldiers, Catalan is often easy to read. *Privat* means private, a *pol* is a pole, and a *bol* is a bowl. But it's confusing. It often cuts off the last consonant of Spanish: *estacion* (station) is *estacio*, *aproximacion* is *aproximacio*. Other times, it adds a consonant that you have to pronounce: *Argeles*, a beach town in French Catalonia, should be pronounced by both French and Spanish with a silent "s." But everybody here pronounces the final "s." Because it's Catalan.

All of this is merely interesting and amusing until you are faced with an all-Catalan menu, as we were for Sunday tapas. Though hungry, I pulled out my new Catalan dictionary (the Spanish one is just getting dusty) and looked up the mystery words:

embotit: "A kind of sausage."

botifarra: "A kind of sausage."

llonganissa: "A kind of sausage."

salsitxa: "A kind of sausage."

And then there were six words meaning *chorizo*. which is … a kind of sausage.

Finally we ordered *Patates Braves* (fierce potatoes), and *Queso Manxega*, which we interpreted as cheese puffs because *manxa* means "bellows." We're trying, okay?

We knew the Fierce Potatoes were fries with Russian dressing, but it turns out the Manxega was Manchego cheese, served with bread smeared with tomato, a beloved Catalan snack. We tried too hard on that one.

We are both baffled. Tom came here to learn Spanish by immersion, but nobody's speaking Spanish. I came here with a total of 102 years of Romance language education stuffed into my brain. Neither one of us knows what's going on.

Still, in only a week, we've absorbed a lot of Catalan. Maybe when Catalonia takes over the world, there will be a need for skilled Yankee interpreters. That's what we're working towards.

Or maybe just being able to order lunch.

Chapter 16: Subdural Hematoma

Now things start to get interesting. I don't want you to read too far in this narrative believing our adventure was all happy travels and smiley faces. Here's my post from May 6, 2013. The event described occurred April 22:

−§−

I open my eyes to a Niagara of gauzy pastel blues and yellows, softly waving in the air. Appropriately, a waterfall of cacophonous Catalan chatter sprays my ears. I am entangled by intubation.

It is visiting hour at Josep Trueta hospital in Girona, Spain, where I am awaiting the prognosis of what has initially been diagnosed as a *subdural hematoma*, which is doc-talk for a clot of blood under the dura mater that covers my brain. The pressure is incessant. There is pain. They conduct a CT scan and tell me clot is the size of a deck of cards.

Yesterday, while I was quietly reading on the balcony at our hotel room at L'Escala, a sudden, sharp pain appeared behind my right eye. I tried to walk it off, to no avail. Finally, I confessed the obvious: Louise called for an ambulance and here I am, hematoma and all, in a very nice hospital (named, interestingly, after the man who invented the plaster cast). This is the Intensive-Care Ward, so I'm keeping company with a dozen patients in similar conditions of distress, separated by the pastel blue and yellow curtains mentioned above. Everyone is speaking, loudly and to my ears, unintelligibly. The headache, blissfully, is gone. So, I hope, is the hematoma.

Surgery is the Hail-Mary pass for this malady. As it's described by my handsome Spanish neurosurgeon (the term "McDreamy" comes to mind) it's not a comforting thought, requiring power tools commonly found in a home workshop. (I thought I heard the words "Black and Decker," but with the accent, perhaps not.) Hoping to avoid mechanized intervention, McDreamy is trying to "dissolve" the hematoma with medication, which is far preferable to garage mechanics. Time will tell.

Thus begins an experiment with expat healthcare. I've been told the Spanish version is excellent (and free if you're a Spanish taxpayer, which I am not). This will be an interesting fiscal experiment, which I will report on these pages, assuming I live long enough to pay the bill.

Aside from the unwitting central character, there are three significant players on stage today:

Jordi Perez Bovet, my neurosurgeon (he should have been a cardiologist, with his heart-melting Cary-Grant accent and looks — a man who once told me "I learned English from Hollywood movies").

Nadia Lorite, Jordi's assistant, whose sweet brown eyes and morning "Hola!" prove that there really *is* a better way of waking up than Folgers in your cup.

My lovely Louise — laughing, adapting (she collects languages the way she collects shoes — and that's a compliment), charming everyone she meets. All this in spite of the pesky scirocco named Tom that blows about her feet and continually threatens her equanimity.

Here in the sands of the Spanish Costa Brava, I have found these three gems. This event would be as unbearable as ... well ... brain surgery, if they weren't looking after my well-being. I am blessed.

Muchas gracias, mis tres amigos.

As for the hematoma, I suspect there will be more to follow.

Chapter 17: The Line Forms at the Door

Matters became a bit more complicated a few days later. The post below appeared on May 7, 2013. The events described occurred April 23rd:

−§−

The hematoma didn't dissolve. Msrs. Black and Decker were summoned. McDreamy approached the project with the enthusiasm of Bob the Builder fresh from a clearance sale at Lowe's. The incision exceeds two feet in length; there are forty-one staples. Half of my skull was removed (and then replaced, much to my satisfaction). It's a good thing chain saws weren't on sale.

McDreamy says I will recover; that mine was a simple procedure in spite of its appearance; and that the hematoma is gone. The culprit, it seems, was medication that was prescribed following last summer's heart attack. (I've had many of those; my cardiologist's number is on speed dial.)

My head is shaved, perforated, and inelegantly stapled. I look like a poster child for a children's cancer charity. Thus, there will be many hats. I have even learned how to tie a do-rag. I now belong to that most exclusive of clubs: men who can tie either a do-rag or a bow-tie from raw fabric.

The line forms at the door, ladies.

−§−

It really *was* a simple procedure. Within five days I was cleared for release from the hospital. Louise had arrived with my street clothes and I was about to walk out the door, when...

Chapter 18: No Sh*t Sherlock!

...well, read for yourself. This is my blog entry for May 8th, 2013. The event described occurred April 30th :

–§–

I counted fourteen gowned sycophants in the room, buzzing about a solitary, supine individual like bees in a hive. At their center – it chafes my sensibilities to type this – playing the role of the queen, was me.

(This is a story of medical complications following major surgery. It's not rare: the removal of half of one's skull certainly qualifies as malevolent trauma, and malevolent trauma is contraindicated when one is trying to keep a querulous heart in his chest.)

I tend to pay acute attention to language when fourteen people are asking questions with the urgency of determined medical professionals. "Tomás, does the crushing pressure around your chest feel familiar?" "Tomás, are those your real teeth?" "Tomás, tell me if you can feel this four-foot piece of adhesive tape that I'm unwrapping from around your hairy chest."

I came to Spain for immersion language learning, and today I found a compelling program. The precision of language – and the need for the learning thereof – is quite apparent when the instructor is aiming a four-inch syringe at your left carotid artery.

In the middle of this carnage, an intense young face appears three inches in front of mine. With incongruous charm, he drops the H-bomb:

"Tomás, you are having a heart attack."

After 45 minutes of hysteria-with-hyperdermics, the only retort that came to mind was the phrase I've used as the title for this chapter, borne of a punitive desire to impart a language lesson of my own: "That's an American idiom, my friend, we have lots of them and most are about as endearing as that hair you just removed from my chest."

It is not my intention to disparage expat healthcare – especially the healthcare that I've received in Spain. Most of the Catalan healthcare professionals I've met received their training here at Josep Trueta University Hospital; it's distinguished by intensely sympathetic eye contact and gentle touches — as endemic to the Catalan psyche as an exaggerated sense of irony is to the American.

In addition to some language, I've learned a few things about expat healthcare that may be of interest to my fellow expats:

Travel with printed records of your medications, if you're on any, and other significant medical data — like who to call in case of emergency, doctor's name, and your height and weight in local units of measurement (anesthesiologists can be so picky...).

Leave home with enough money (or credit) in the bank to pay the bill with a simple debit- or credit-card transaction or a wire transfer. This may not be as bad as it sounds: the bill for my experience — brain surgery and a heart attack — was about $21,000 US. A single heart attack in Portland last August cost almost twice that amount. More often than not, healthcare outside of the US is a bargain — but only if you can cover the cost yourself until your insurance company can reimburse you. It's a dear commitment, but hopefully you will be reimbursed by insurance, and settling up with your insurance company is best done when you're away from the discharge desk, where they can always send you back to your room.

Count your blessings and take them home with you. I made good friends while I was in the hospital. A lovely watercolor of the Girona Cathedral was given to me by my English-club friend Steve Brown, who also smuggled Coke into my room when I was most parched. Gerard Stutje in the neighboring room visited every day, lent me his Formula 1 magazine as a Spanish-language learning aid, and invited me over to watch Moto GP on his dime (at Josep Trueta Hospital, you pay for TV by the hour). Friends like Steve and Gerard are an estimable measure of wealth. So is an appreciation of the professionals I mentioned earlier who expressed genuine compassion about my well-being. Given the value of passionate humanity (and the ephemeral quality of money), I believe I actually made a profit while I was hospitalized.

Don't chuck your Kindle into the laundry basket. In a moment of misplaced sports loyalties, one of the nurses — a Pancho-Villa sort of fellow, full of hail and fare-thee-well — and I sparred over a *fútbol* match between Barcelona (me) and Madrid (Pancho). (Warning to travelers: Spanish enthusiasm for fútbol is contagious.) My Kindle was cradled on a chair heaped with dirty laundry; Pancho unintentionally wadded it all into a ball and — *goooooooooal!* — chucked the whole enchilada into the laundry basket (use of hands — red card). The good news: Amazon Spain was able to overnight a new Kindle. The bad news: Barcelona lost.

I emerge from this event unmistakably bald, slightly more multilingual, and very much endowed with an appreciation for humanity. I could lament lost days and hospital food, but I rejoice instead: I'm alive and I'm in love with a whole new nation of amigos and compañeros.

¡La vida está bien!

Chapter 19: A Letter From Louise

After I had returned from the hospital for a few days, Louise emailed a letter to me that she had written while I was away. I cry every time I read it. You may too.

—§—

My Darling,

I will start with today. Today you were angry or perhaps sad. I cannot blame you for this. You have been violated, accidentally and on purpose.

You have always been handsome, but today you were even more so. The chain mail helmet that goes around the top of your head and under your chin makes you look like medieval knight. You have long been my savior in shining armor, and today you really looked like that.

But it is made of gauze, beneath it a wound turban, white with a sporty red stripe, that covers the place where they broke into your skull with a saw and started to drain out the thin blood that had settled there, pressing on your brain. Today I could see the blood, leaking out into a clear plastic bulb on your pillow.

I squeeze your hand, I talk to you. Today you woke up and squeezed back. You said "I miss you," and asked if you had had surgery. You complained about your bad dreams ("a chamber of horrors") and the occasional violent tremor of your left hand, and you said you wanted to go home. You wanted cava and ice cream. You wanted to get out of there. You said you had had a bad night. You said "Some vacation in Spain. This is not what I planned."

Your complaints might have seared my heart, except that you are well enough to complain. It is not like you to complain, but I sure do get it. You have every right; you are in a state of shock physically and every other way, but you have the good sense to complain. This is wonderful.

You don't know where you have been, do you?

So now, about yesterday.

April 24th, 2013 I arrived at the hospital at 10 a.m., only mildly agitated. The night before you were so up and on the way to better. But this morning, well, this morning you are asleep with your Kindle in hand and your old bear on your chest. I make a little noise which is usually enough to wake you, but no. I reach over and grab your hand, stroke your face. Your beautiful blue eyes open and stare at me and you say nothing.

But I think, he is sleepy. He hasn't eaten or drunk in two days. His blood sugar is low. The hopeful things we tell ourselves! At last you speak: "What have you been doing today?"

I say: "So far I just did the wash."

"The what?"

"The wash. Clothes."

"What did you wash?"

"The dirty clothes from our trip."

Your head goes somewhere else, like you don't know what trip. We talk some more but it seems messages take a very long time to get to you, and the answers are not always the answers to the questions. I can almost see the misfiring.

The night before, you had said, "I keep thinking about that movie, *l'Amour*, where the woman couldn't pour coffee into her cup."

I said: "I remember that she was staring into space."

And today you say, after a pause, "Am I staring into space?"

Suddenly you begin to laugh at some inner joke. Finally, you point to Bear. "Chick magnet." You smile.

You reach for your phone, and say, "I'll read you the post I wrote for the next blog entry." You need to find it; your fingers have trouble finding the right buttons to push. Yesterday you wrote this amazing, mellifluous, fantastic report of life in the emergency room in Spain, seeing it as yet another adventure, and today you can barely find the buttons to call it up. Finally you do, and begin to read haltingly.

Slowly it is dawning on me that this is not low blood sugar. Your left hand is trembling a little. I start to cry, for the first time. And I don't know what to do. Is it time to sound an alarm? To rush into the corridor and scream for help? This is not my Tom. Bring back my Tom.

At that moment, Dr. Perez comes in with a woman whom we later know as his helper, Nadia. He looks at you. You stare. "How are you doing?" he asks.

He looks at me, and I just slowly shake my head. Not good. Not good. I try to explain that you have lost your spirit, that your thoughts do not connect, that your brain is working through petroleum jelly, slowly, struggling.

He has you lift your arms. Obediently you went through the rest of the drill without being asked, finger to nose, lift right leg, lift left leg. The doctor is only looking at your trembling left hand. He speaks Catalan with the woman who is with him, urgently. And then he looks at me. "This is a complication. I think we will have to do the surgery today. This morning."

We both talked to you about this, and you stare. It is not clear that you get it. It doesn't matter because we had already signed the release for it in advance. So this is how it happens. The surgery happens when the patient no longer knows what's happening.

The doctor leaves, I cry again, Steve Brown from the Girona Grapevine pops in the door. "Oh look, Tom, it's Peter," I say. "Steve," says Steve. You stare.

"Steve from the English speaking group, Tom."

You stare and grin the way you do when you can't hear what's happening but want to appear friendly anyway. It is not clear if you know what's happening. But yes, he mentions the newsletter and there is a gleam of recognition about the fact that you wrote something for it, and Steve is grateful. We even talk about the Mercedes newsletter that I made you edit.

I explain that we have just decided on surgery. "I'll walk you to the door," I say. And outside the door I start to cry again, apologizing, and Steve is all good. "Anything we can do," he says. "We don't know you, but we feel that we know you." He has already sent an email telling me I can talk to the British Benevolence woman in Girona, and that we are honorary Brits. Sweet.

The Doogie Hauser-young Dr. Jordi Perez Bovet explains again that the surgery is serious, but simple ("sample") and routine. He says you are young and in good health and that will help your chances to heal and to heal fast. He says "Do not worry. Do not worry. Do NOT worry." I am of course crying. You look at me and say, "That's a lot of do not worries," I say. "I guess he means it."

Staff piles into the room to jab you with IVs, pump plasma in. You cannot make a fist and I do it for you. After the IV is in you cannot get the message to undo the fist, and I do it for you.

We take off your wedding ring. After a minute you say, "It's tungsten. It won't affect the machines." My Tom is in there. He is deep within there, but he is there.

I follow you to the hall outside surgery, trailed by a lovely woman named Merces who wants to know about our insurance coverage. They need pre-authorization from Blue Cross. It is 1:00 a.m. on the West Coast, but I call anyway, and am told to call in office hours, please. After some hesitation, the Spaniards agree to go ahead with the surgery anyway. We must save your beautiful brain.

I go back to you. "I just signed on for general anesthesia," you say, looking scared. I know you fear anesthesia. And then you say, "Am I going in for a cat scan?"

And I tell you it's all going to be okay. But not knowing that. The anesthesiologists corner me to say quite solemnly, that because you have had heart attacks and strokes, you may have a heart attack or stroke. Previously, Dr. Perez had read us the obligatory list of possible complications, all of them bad. Death was in there. Paralysis, too. Brain damage, of course. "But a less than ten percent chance of any of that."

So off you go. I wish they would give me some anesthesia too, and only wake me when my Tom comes back. If.

The surgery will take two to four hours, and I am told not to worry if I don't hear from them for five hours or more. That is normal. I figure I will walk home, loosen the joints, get air, try to import some happy chemicals from the exercise. And I call Jeannette because I am way too alone and scared. I tell her I am walking home.

I walk maybe a half mile, and then realize it is a bad idea. You are not having knee surgery. You are having brain surgery. I need to be close. I even need to be near your energy, and maybe you need mine. You are much more alone than I am.

I turn around and go back to the waiting room. I alternate between reading my novel, praying, playing gin against my phone, and praying some more. And more.

Finally Vicens and Jeannette arrive and they both come over and immediately hug me before hello, and I am in tears all over again. Vicens stays in the waiting room and Jeannette and I go to the cafeteria and she makes me eat something. I am not hungry, but I do. She is sitting with Bear at a table when I bring my tray. She asks questions and talks. I ask her if you will be the same Tom. Of course, as everyone is always saying, nothing is guaranteed. But when the blood stops pressing on the brain, the brain returns to its normal shape and presumably function.

And then, we go back to the surgery waiting room where Vicens has been marking my place, waiting for news.

Finally, two medical folk come out, I've never seen them before. They deliver rapid fire Catalan, and I look lost while Vicens and Jeannette nod. They tell me this: the surgery went well. The clot was small, but in two places. You have gone to intensive care, and I must wait more. Vicens and Jeanette have to go to work, they say goodbye.

The intensive care chief (man with pointy beard who sort of speaks English) beckons me into a scary sparsely furnished room which they must use to tell people The Worst. He reiterates, but very solemnly, that all went well, and that there would possibly be only "minimal brain damage."

Minimal? I am stunned. I have seen your slow thinking and your flailing left arm. "Minimal?" I ask. "What about none?"

He reflects on this. "Minimal, or none." I later reflect that in translation, minimal may mean minimal or none. But at the time, it was petrifying.

He tells me what I can expect to see: a sleeping person wearing lots of equipment. They are keeping the sedation going a bit longer because....I don't know why.

He tells me to wait in the waiting room for the next step. Finally, an older woman attendant comes out and brings me in to an anteroom, miming instructions. Here I put on a green gown with the number six on it. I am told to put my purse in a locker with the number six on it. This is all because you are in box number six. I'm not kidding. Box Six.

Rather terrified at this point, I follow her to Box Six. You are fast asleep, snoring loudly, and sometimes just stopping, not breathing. You are wearing an enormous white gauze turban. There is a breathing tube in your mouth, a tube coming out from beneath which is dripping watery blood into a clear bulb. You look nearly dead. I feel like you've been lobotomized. I stare, I watch, I listen, nurses stare sympathetically and bustle. I can't stay long, because I can't stand seeing this. I know you're not going to wake up. Too hard to see this. If all goes well, this is the worst you will ever look.

The Insurance Lady is waiting for me outside, and drags me down to her office to try and call Blue Cross again. I first hear a warning that this is NOT a toll free number from abroad, and them I am on hold, then I am explaining what I need, on hold again. I hear bad jazz and endless recorded helpful tips about my health.

The woman at the other end must be working at home; there is a shrieking cat in the background. She is slow. She finds the policy and reads from it, the terms of the hospital bill. As for the payment for surgery, she can't guarantee anything until she sees the bill. We are more than a week away from the bill. The hospital needs assurance that we have insurance.

She puts me on hold so she can find the address for Blue Cross Global, where the bill and claim should go. We are paying about $10 a minute for me to listen to bad jazz for probably another five minutes. I am sweating and the Insurance Lady wants to go home. I finally hang up and convince the Insurance Lady that I will go home and keep working on it. She gives me until Friday.

So I leave, and I think, walked all the way back. I don't remember. I keep checking my phone and realize it is telling me it needs more money. This is not good, as I must have a line ready for any call from the hospital. I visit the grocery to buy strawberries and vodka and ask about refilling the phone, and she sends me to the ATM machine. It makes all the right noises but refuses to help.

I get to the dental clinic and ask Adriana to help. She tries hard. Doesn't have an Orange phone. Suspects I ought to go to the Orange store. Bad news, that. Always busy, and only one person speaks English and he is not always there. And I am a wreck.

Then she says Vicens has rearranged his evening appointments so he can drive me to the hospital for the 8 p.m. visit. This is astonishing.

I go upstairs and send out the email that describes your setback and your sudden surgery. It is still 8 a.m. at home. I don't know what else happened.

At 7 p.m., Adrianna calls to say Vicens is ready. Then she talks him into taking me to the Orange store, which he does. We have to wait for ten minutes or so, and the English person is not on duty, but Vicens quickly has it all sorted out.

Then he drives me to the hospital, and I tell him he can leave me but he won't. He sits with me in the waiting room and I am so anxious that I don't know what to say or how.

I go in for the green gown, etc. I dread what I will see this time. You are still sleeping and snoring, the breathing tube gone, breathing on your own now. Your left eye is a tad open and I wonder if it is open or shut and if you can see me. I talk to you but you cannot hear me. They tell me to speak slowly and softly. I rub your shoulder to try to wake you up. Doesn't work.

The nurses apologize for the restraints on your wrists, but said that when you awoke you got agitated and sat up straight and wanted to go pipi and wanted to go home. You were ready to just rip out of bed. "He spoke?" I asked.

"Yes!" they say.

"Did it make sense?"

Now they are silent, wiggling their flat palms, meaning, oh, sort of.

Now the pointy-bearded doctor comes in and whacks you on the shoulder a few times and shouts.

"TOM! TOM! Wake up! Look who's here!"

I feel really bad for you. Stop whacking him!

Finally he shouts, "HOW DO YOU FEEL?"

You open your cracked lips and croak: "Muy bien."

And go back to sleep.

Coming out of there, I bump right into Vicens and burst into tears again. He's okay with this.

He brings me home and then I write to everybody that you spoke Spanish to the doctor, which has to be a good sign. I ask for more prayers.

What I don't know is if you will be partly paralyzed, or brain damaged, and if so, in what way. Dick calls and I tell him all the bad stuff, and burst into tears again. He is good about it.

Alec and Ted both offer to Skype, but I tell them it's hard to talk to a crying woman, and we will talk when all is calmer. And finally I sleep, setting an alarm because I will want to see you at the 7:15 visit. I am so eager to know if you are still In There.

April 22nd I know you don't remember exactly what happened, so we'll go back to the sunny Monday in L'Escala when you were reading at siesta time. Then you asked me if I had an ibuprofen. I did not. You said you had a big gigantic and sudden headache in the back of your right eye.

We embarked on our evening walk anyway, but you turned back to go lie down. I went off in pursuit of ibuprofen and finally found a farmacia. When I got back to the hotel you were really kind of dopey and dizzy and lying down. I gave you the pills and you couldn't quite grasp them, but we got them down. You seemed to be slipping and said you couldn't really walk.

I went down to the front desk and told the woman there that we needed medical help of some kind. She said the hospital was next door and we could walk there, but you couldn't. She made a phone call and was rebuffed by someone who said there are no ambulances or housecalls for headaches. She made another phone call and this time an ambulance arrived.

Back upstairs, every system in your body seemed to be failing. You were nauseous, profoundly weak, and in terrible brain pain. I paced and fretted. I could see this was serious but there was nothing I could do.

Two young EMTs finally nearly broke the door down to get to you, asking questions: where was your passport, your medical card, what were the symptoms, what were you allergic to, where is your medication list. The woman EMT is now asking me what medicine I gave you, what I asked for at the farmacia, why did you give him medication recommended by a pharmacist instead of a doctor? I thrust at her the flyer that came with the medication. Now she begins to read the warnings aloud to the group, with dagger glances at me between sentences. Drama queen.

Can you sit up? Huh? With help, you can. Immediately you start to vomit and a trash can is brought. It's on the sheets, the hotel lady says not to worry about that. They give you a plastic bag to clutch and eventually a stretcher comes in, you're stuffed into the ambulance, and off we go.

The L'Escala Hospital is just around the block. You go right into the emergency department where we go through all the questions again. Two nurses are very calm, and so is a doctor who seems to be Indian but who speaks Spanish. You get one shot, right cheek, for the pain, and one shot, left cheek, for the nausea. In order to do this, the two of us have to roll you each way because you can't move easily, nor process the instructions.

Then the Indian Spanish doctor tells me you're going to the Girona hospital because they have a very good eye department. At the moment we are focusing on the previous stroke that knocked out your right eye; that's where the pain is.

"I didn't poison him?" I ask, put out by the issue with the OTC pain medication.

He shakes his head, no, no, no. A foolish idea, even.

We all bundle back into the ambulance and take off for Girona. The drama queen EMT is at the wheel and we don't talk much on the way. I am terrified that what seemed like a headache is hitting every system in your body. The driver and the man EMT in the back talk to each other a little but all is silence from you.

The driver explains that the L'Escala hospital is not equipped for this, that Figueres is only 20 minutes, but there was a chance we would be sent on to Girona from there, so why not go the extra ten minutes to the best hospital?

I ask if the Girona hospital is expecting you, and she says she doesn't think anybody called ahead.

I am thinking, "Don't we have to hurry?"

You are disembarked on your stretcher and swallowed up into the inner sanctum of the emergency room and I am sent out to the waiting room to register you. Your passport is back at the hotel, we never knew about the Europe health card, but your driver's license and Blue Cross card seem to be adequate, along with the list of medications you usually take.

I am to sit and wait. I read, I pace. All around me are worried people, other people rushing in with sick children, many in Arab dress. I catch a glimpse of one of my EMTs leaving the hospital. "Que pasa?"

He says he doesn't really know. They have looked at you and now you are waiting.

Every hour I go to the desk and ask what's happening. They tell me to wait, I will be called . And after three hours, I am.

The emergency ward is full of people on gurneys, in little rooms, in hallways. You are in a smallish room behind a curtain. You speak foggily, but the painkiller has taken effect. I look around and the floor is filthy.

The edges where the linoleum floor meets the wall are grimy black, and there are dust bunnies all around. There is no chair, so I try to sit on the floor, but it's too awful. Eventually, I will steal a chair from across the hall.

You are foggy, but you know what's happening. Someone comes to get you for a chest x-ray, then brings you back. Someone comes to get you for a brain MRI, then brings you back. A woman comes in and says "Your heart is okay, but there is blood in your brain."

Then we see Jordi Perez Bovet for the first time. He explains that he is a neurosurgeon (*a neurosurgeon!*) and this is a subdural hematoma, and what that is, and that you will have to be admitted for treatment. He goes away and then somebody comes back and hustles you away again for another MRI. Only when we get outside the room does the transpo man explain that we are getting another picture. Now things are going faster. They are in a hurry.

Now Jordi reappears in your dust bunny-infested ER stall. He says the subdural hematoma is the result of overly-thinned blood, and our conservative approach will be to see if it goes away by itself. You will be given a kind of cortisone that might resolve the problem in a few days.

Then he brings in a consent to surgery. "We don't plan on doing surgery, but we will want to if this doesn't clear up by itself. It means cutting out a piece of skull, flushing the puddle of blood, and vacuuming it up. Then we put the flap back and sew it all back together. It is simple. It is common surgery.

"But of course I must tell you the risks. The anesthesia always carries a risk. Because we are near the brain, there is a risk of brain damage, infection, paralysis, heart attack, seizures, and of course, death. These risks have only a ten percent chance, they are not likely, but I must tell you. The risks of not doing the surgery are the same, but the chances are much higher.

"So will you agree to it?" He puts a pen in your hand. We look at each other, and you sign. I have to sign it too.

You are wheeled upstairs to room upstairs 726. You are forbidden food and drink in case of the need for surgery, and you are hooked up with intravenous tubes. Dr. Jordi says that during this time we will be watching for any change in your condition, especially a dip in consciousness or a physical irregularity on the left side.

You ask me to contact a list of people, the kids and close friends. It is four in the morning when I leave you and take a cab home. They call one for me from the emergency room.

April 23rd On this day I found the bus stop and went to the hospital early. You were alert, you were talking, you were making sense. You were not in pain. I went back later and you were the same. I went home and sent encouraging messages to the people back home. I thought, okay, this is going to work. He'll be back soon.

Great messages of love and concern come back.

And then the next day, you had turned into an old man: forgetful, deaf, blind, and slow. I thought I would never see my Tom again. Well, I suddenly knew that was possible, and I knew what it would be like, because you were acting it out right in front of me.

April 25th On the day after the surgery, I was allowed three visits, the first at 7:15. Now there were a group of us, waiting on the second floor lobby, and called in a few at a time. The green gown, the locked up purse, the handwashing, and on to Box Six. They have taken out the breathing tube and you look vaguely less pathetic, but still rather grainy.

You talk to me, and suddenly your left hand begins a violent tremble. You reach over with your right hand and try to calm it, I do the same.

At the noon visit, the Dr. Jordi appeared and said: "He's going to be all right."

Alright is such a vague word. Alright in the head, but paralyzed on the left side? Walking and talking alright but slow in the head? My wonderful funny loving caring genius but in a wheelchair?

"Do you mean 100%?" I ask.

"100%," he says. "The only thing is, there are seizures in the left arm. So we are giving him anti-seizure medication and he will have to take that for a long time, maybe forever. They will not hurt him, and he will have no seizures while he keeps taking it."

April 26th Your gauze cap is off. I had tried to see how long the scar was by peering under it before. Now I see that it snakes around from the front of your ear almost to the back of your head, then up to the crown and forwards to the hairline. Or what used to be the hairline. It is an angry red, with 41 staples, and the additional insult of a sloppy line of rust-colored Betadine. It looks awful.

The left of your head is covered with all your normal lovely silver hair. From that side you look like yourself.

This is the day I asked Vicens in with his clipping machine. It just seemed sensible — less weird — to take off the rest of your hair. I started the job, but he finished it. You were giddy and made a movie of it. At the end you looked less weird. Next visit, I brought you a bandanna.

April 29th I arrive at about 11 a.m., and you jubilantly tell me you are going home tomorrow. Yay!

At the noon visit, Dr. Jordi checks you out, observes your wellness and your willingness, and says, why not, let's send you home today.

The Ghanaian psychic woman with the mop, ebony in color, tells you you won't go home today. Nonsense. The nurse asks if he has clothes to go. The weather is rainy and cold. You have only boxers and pants. No shirt, no jacket. I go home to get them, stopping on the way home for beer and sausages and ingredients for the cassoulet you want when you get home.

I arrive at the hospital with all your gear, and you are standing in the hall. "Hey, how are you?"

"Dreadful," you say. "Pain all over."

I stuff you back into bed but you keep getting up. I run out in the hall and tell nurse Paula there's a problem. "Big or small?" she asks.

"Big," I say.

The staff returns from lunch at 3 p.m., all atwitter. Suddenly, Dr. Jordi is in the room, begging for an EKG machine. The room fills with people, and I am sent to the hall. Runners come and go returning with vials and medicines and machines from all parts of the floor. More and more nurses, med students, and doctors arrive. Once they call for the cardiologist, I pretty much know what's happening.

I am almost relieved when they say "heart attack" because we have been through those before.

I think you know the rest.

Welcome back!

Chapter 20: Ay Ay Guapos!

Life went on. Recovery was slow but without surprises. We did not return to the USA. People often express surprise when we tell them that we continued with the adventure, but really: what was the difference? Recover in the USA (where we had no home), or recover in Spain (where we had an apartment and loving friends)? Besides, Girona is nested in the land of cava (Spanish sparkling wine), which was as inexpensive as Mogan-David but remarkably refreshing, so cava helped me along. There's no feeling sorry for yourself when a nearby glass brims with festive bubbles. Note to Catalan doctors: prescribe cava for recovery. There's no better medicine.

But I digress. Life went on, and in Girona, life means the street market. In a post dated May 14th, 2013, Louise describes ours:

—§—

My guilty pleasure is street markets. I absolutely haunt the one in the park next door: La Devesa.

This market shows up every Tuesday and Saturday morning, and for some reason I always see things I haven't seen before.

Unlike all other markets I've seen, this one has aggressive barkers. These are usually men behind the display tables who are shouting:

Ay Ay Ay! (Translation: Ay Ay Ay!)

Guapas! (You beautiful women!)

Marcas de calidad! (Quality brands!)

Tots tres euros! (Everything three euros!)

Barato! (Cheap!)

At the same time, the barkers are scrutinizing every potentially sticky finger in the mad scramble for scarves, striped teeshirts, voile tunics, bed slippers, and harem pants, making sure that nobody slips a *marca de calidad* into her rollerbag without handing over the three euros. This dual skill is surely something that is passed from one generation to the next. You can't be a man until you can shout "Marcas de calidad!" and really sound like you mean it.

Maybe it's a cultural thing, but I tend to shy away from the calidad barkers. Being a native New Englander, I much prefer marketplaces where the vendor gives you a chilly nod when you walk in and then goes back to reading *Leaves of Grass*. Or places like a Chanel store, where they sort of stare you down if they suspect your credit maxes out at $15,000.

But enough. What can you buy at my market? Garlic presses, baskets, bikinis, fry pans, scarves by the bushel, Chinese jewelry, espadrilles, sequinned teeshirts, hammers and nails, suitcases, toys, gardening tools, those polyester pull-on trousers that are worn by 80-year-olds worldwide, crocheted vests, lace tops, tights, jeans, belts, (gosh, I wish I were being paid by the word, or paid at all....) plants, hot dogs, jeggings, housesdresses, purses, wallets, backpacks, teeshirts with nonsense phrases in English, and — *TA-DA!* — wedding gowns (60 euros; assortment on display). Although that stall actually has more cocktail dresses (40 euros.)

Now you probably want to know what I have actually bought. Comfy black espadrilles, a big yellow not-quite-leather backpack, and Super Glue. But who knows what I'll find on Saturday?

Chapter 21: Geeky Good Things

Travel brought many useful skills. While Louise was perfecting her shopping technique, I was honing packing lists, uploading blog entries, and optimizing my hard drive—you know: useful, productive tasks. The entry I wrote below was one of our most popular posts, dated May 27, 2013:

—§—

Does Martha Stewart still say, "It's a good thing"? Hearing her say that on her TV show soured me on the expression forever, yet there are so many occasions when I could use the phrase. This is one of them.

Warning: geeky stuff ahead, but useful geeky stuff. Especially if you travel to far-away lands. Below is a list of tech solutions that travel with us and have proven to be indispensable. I'll be brief.

- **Kindles**. We each have one, what Amazon calls the "Paperwhite" model. They glow in the dark (from within, somewhat magically) so you can read them in bed without disturbing your partner, and they're easy to read out of doors, the more sunlight the better. Kindles hold over a thousand books (whatever for?) and weigh a little over half a pound. They're about as thick as a pack of matches. Kindle books (buy them with the Kindle itself wherever WiFi is around) are often available for free and those that do cost money almost always cost less than their respective printed versions.
- **Battery-powered USB charger**. Speaking of Kindles, they are battery powered and since they discharge so infrequently (about every two weeks), you sometimes forget to charge them and get the critical-battery message just when there are ten pages remaining in a Baldacci novel. What to do? Plug it into the wall outlet? You're in bed, Sherlock. The wires are in the other room, the outlet is down near the floor, and the wires will probably strangle (or electrocute) you as you fall asleep anyway. The solution is a battery USB charger. It's just

a big battery (relatively speaking—mine's about the size of a salt shaker) that you plug your Kindle (or phone, or camera) into so you can keep on doing whatever it was that you were doing in the first place. What's more, it will operate and charge your device while it's connected. Mine will charge my phone twice before it needs to be charged itself. No more long wires in inconvenient places at inopportune times!

- **High-power, multiple-outlet, dual-voltage USB charger**. When you must plug things into the wall to charge them, a high-power USB charger is the solution. Mine retracts its plug for convenient storage, and offers two one-amp (or 1,000 milliamp, considered "high power") USB connections. Oh sure, you can charge things like phones with the USB connection on your computer, but that's usually rated at 250 to 500 milliamps, thus requiring as much as four times as long to do the job. Get an adapter and be sure the one you select is rated for both American (110v) and European voltage (220v). I've noticed that a lot of things that require charging via USB cable no longer come with a USB adapter (just a cable), so as long as you're gonna have to get something anyway, get one of these.

- **European outlet adapter**. We carry three or four of these, suitable for European outlets. There are others for UK and Australian outlets. They don't change the voltage, they just change the pin configuration. They're cheap, and since everything you're traveling with is rated for both 110 and 220 volts (it is, isn't it?), all you need are the right holes in the right place. I think I bought six of these for about eight dollars.

- **A multiple-outlet power strip**. This is just a version of the old-fashioned extension cord with four or five outlets. The versions optimized for travel have short cords that fold and stow neatly. They're standard 110-volt items; one of the adapters described above is all that's necessary: plug the adapter into the wall; plug the power strip into the outlet and you have four (or more) US-style outlets. Ours is a Monster "Outlets-to-Go" power strip. There are many others.

Virtual Private Network. This is especially geeky,
‍‌t worth whatever it takes. A Virtual Private Network
(VPN) is a way to spoof trolls who eavesdrop on public
network traffic in places like Starbucks, where the harvest
is sometimes account numbers and passwords. You'd never
want to log into your bank, for example, when you're using
a public network. Instead, you route your data through a
VPN and the trolls are foiled.

A side benefit is that many VPNs are in the US, so
anything you're connected to thinks you're in the States, no
matter where you really are.

Let's take Netflix. If Netflix determines you're outside
of the US (where they don't have the necessary licenses),
you'll probably get a message saying that their service isn't
available in your location—and no Netflix. Ditto Pandora
and scores of other entertainment sites. My VPN is in
Florida, I think. It's software. There's nothing to buy. And it
works. Google "VPN."

Everything I've mentioned (except the Kindles) fits into a small
zippered bag. The bag and everything in it is an essential to travel
nowadays (if you have phones or cameras), and quite inexpensive.
It's a Good Thing.

I'll deny I said that if you ever quote me.

$-\S-$

And while we're on the subject of Tips for Travelers, here's an
excerpt from a post dated June 6th, 2013, where I discussed the
technique we used to get our mail:

$-\S-$

Even though we're in Girona for three months, that really isn't
enough time to change our mailing address. Not officially, and not
when we're about to move again in three weeks.

Instead, we use my daughter's mailing address in the States. She looks at our mail as it arrives and writes a quick email if anything appears to be of specific interest. (This doesn't happen very often: in this electronic age, where we do our banking, pay our bills, and accomplish almost everything else via the Internet, USPS mail rarely presents anything of interest.)

If we email back and say she should examine a specific letter, she opens it, takes a picture of it with her phone, and emails the picture. Emailing pictures is something she does all the time (she's Gen-X, after all), and the pictures are clear enough for us to determine what we want to do next.

That's it. At least for us, mail is that simple.

Chapter 22: Moving On

Our stay in Girona was drawing to a close. As "serial expats" we were destined to move on to another temporary home. This provoked lots of emotion, which I discussed in this post dated June 27th, 2013:

$-\S-$

"Meet us under the big clock at the railroad station."

When our friend Simone suggested that meeting place, we knew exactly where that clock was. We knew how long it would take to walk there. We even knew that at that time of day, the clock would be in the shade. We have lived here three months, and three months is long enough to know things like this.

And now we're about to leave.

How long is three months?

It's long enough to learn nearly all of the geographic landmarks in town—how much of a walk is required to get to each one, and even minutiae like their orientation to the sun—like the big clock.

It's long enough to lose stuff in the apartment: under the bed, in corners blocked off by furniture, in the cupboards under the kitchen counters.

It's long enough to learn how to successfully operate the remotes for the TV and the satellite receiver.

It's long enough to require cleaning of the microwave and refrigerator.

It's long enough to experience an occasional day with no particular desire to get out and see or do anything.

It's long enough to see the trees in the park fully leaf out.

It's long enough for a light bulb in the living room to burn out.

It's long enough to make good friends—and to know we'll regretfully miss them when we leave.

We're packing up. We're searching under the bed, under the counters, and in the corners for those lost socks. We're walking the streets of Girona and seeing familiar sights for what may be the last time. We're sad. We're excited. We're anxious.

Such is the plight of the serial expat: stay long enough to live (and if you're lucky, love) the life, then run off to discover another. During moments like this, pulling up stakes can seem mistaken, when friendships have been made and the dust bunnies have taken up residence.

Perhaps adventure is just that way.

apter 23: Things You Won't Read in the Guidebooks

We arrived in Greece, on the island of Crete in a quaint little town called Chania (HAN-ya) in early July. It was hot but the beauty that surrounded us made us forget all discomfort (besides, our apartment was air-conditioned). We swam in the Mediterranean. We ate Greek food. We hiked the ruins. We were there for a little over three weeks. It wasn't enough.

Below, my post from July 22nd, 2013:

—§—

Two weeks. That's how long we've been in Chania. We've pretty well scoured the city (it's small: population ~55,000) and are now taking an inventory of all the beaches within a day's outing. Louise is learning the language (note the absence of the plural "we"), and we're becoming gourmands, having now visited—oh, I dunno—maybe 500 local restaurants. (Lord, thank you for the food on this island.)

But now, some of the things we've learned (and that you won't read in the guidebooks) about the local culture:

Raki Here in Chania, raki flows like politicians' promises. Many little grocery stores and restaurants produce their own, distilling the skins and stems (pomace) left over after wine production. Sometimes, distillation is done twice, striving to produce an aperitif that's at least 90 proof. In Chania, like Spain, you can occupy a restaurant's table as long as you like—all night if you wish—until you call for the check. When you do, the check is presented along with a little carafe of raki (and, most often, several slices of cold watermelon—all at no charge).

We have been known to quaff our free raki, pay the bill, and trundle off to a waterfront restaurant (where the tourist watching is best) for another carafe. Or two. Double raki nights pretty much preclude doing anything the next day.

English Almost everyone speaks it. Tourists here come primarily from Scandinavia, with a few Germans and Italians representing Europe. None of them speak Greek, so they all fall back on English, which seems to be a common lingual denominator. Coming from Girona, where everyone speaks Catalan and you'd better too, the English we hear around here is a relief.

(Note: Most signage is *not* in English. It's in the Greek language and the Greek alphabet. With Catalan, we could often sound out signage and arrive at meanings; not so in Greece. Try sounding out Ρακί μας είναι η καλύτερη στα Χανιά.)

The VAT Not everything is to love in Greece. The 23% VAT (Value Added Tax) is especially abusive. A twenty-euro dinner is a twenty-five euro dinner as far as we, the consumers, are concerned. That's gotta be especially tough on sellers, who have to fork over almost a quarter of their sales to the government, while all the buyers see is the bottom line. No wonder the Greeks demonstrate!

Black Pants How do you tell the Greek men from the tourists? It's warm here, so most men wear sandals and shorts, but a true Greek wears long pants, usually black (blue jeans too), with socks and shoes, no matter what the weather. Giorgio Armani would be right at home. (In fact, he *was* right at home here a few days ago, having parked his yacht [black, of course] just outside the harbor and wandered ashore to sample a Chania restaurant. We hope he visited Taverna Strata, our favorite.)

The Weather The weather's perfection here is almost monotonous. Every day has been cloudless since we arrived, with temperatures in the mid-eighties, very little wind, and glorious sunsets. It's just right for lazing on the beaches we've been inventorying, which takes me back to the beginning of this post, and perfect closure. Αντίο!

Chapter 24: There Are No Cattle on Crete

As much as we loved Chania and Crete, the Greek culture never failed to bring a smile to our faces with its quirks and foibles. Example: huge Greek weddings. Everyone is invited to Greek weddings: the butcher, the butcher's family, the family next door to the butcher. Of course it's expensive, but tradition says that everyone in attendance gives a monetary gift. No toasters or Cuisinarts, just money. Large donations preferred. Invariably, with so many in attendance, the bride and groom profit in spite of the cost of the wedding. The profits can be immense. It's expected. It's a kickstarter to financial well-being.

Here's another example I posted, from July 27th, 2013:

$$-\S-$$

Greek gun laws change over time, but generally they prohibit the ownership of rifles over 22 caliber. However, as they say in Greece: "everything is prohibited; everything is permitted." That goes especially for Crete, where laws are looked upon as "guides," rather than ... well ... laws. (You oughta see how these people park!)

In other words, there are guns here, many of them rifles larger than 22's. And what do people do for fun with rifles?

Target practice.

Anyone who has practiced with targets can tell you that it quickly provokes the desire for a more challenging experience. In other words, the step from shooting targets to shooting road signs (from a moving vehicle, at night, when the signs reflect headlights) is often looked upon as a natural progression, especially on Crete.

On another topic, the mountains of Crete are infested with feral goats, called *kri-kri*'s. There are so many kri-kri's that the government posts road signs in particularly infested areas warning motorists of kri-kri's in the road.

The kri-kri signs are great for target practice.

Crete long ago gave up on enforcing laws that make it illegal to shoot kri-kri signs, finding it less expensive to simply replace the signs when they become unrecognizable from gunshot holes.

A few years ago, Crete placed an order with Athens for more kri-kri signs. Kri-kri's only live on Crete, Athens didn't have kri-kri signs in stock, so they sent what they had: cattle signs.

There are no cattle on Crete.

Crete said the cattle signs wouldn't do, but Athens found it cheaper to offer the already-shipped cattle signs at a discount than to order up a fresh batch of kri-kri signs. Athens responded to Crete by knocking 50% off the price of the cattle signs.

No Cretan can resist a discount. Crete took the cattle signs.

Which is why the island of Crete has cattle-warning road signs even though there are no cattle on Crete.

I love this place.

Chapter 25: Imprisoned by Our Own Bags

The time came to leave Chania. We bused to Heraklion, Crete's port city, caught an overnight ferry from there to Athens (bunk beds, but fun), and from Athens took another bus to Patras, another port city where we were to catch another overnight ferry to Venice.

If it was all predictable, it wouldn't be adventure, right? And with all the buses, taxis, and boats we had traveled on, there was plenty of opportunity for unpredictability. And snafus. Here's my post from August 7th, 2013:

—§—

We arrived at the Patras ferry terminal at about 11:00 AM Saturday, checked in, and were told that we would be able to board Corragio, our Venice-bound, two-night ferry around 9:00 PM that night for a midnight departure. It was going to be a ten-hour wait, but we knew it was coming.

So far, so good.

We endured the wait, imprisoned by our own bags. The ferry terminal — in most ways quite modern and clean — offered no storage for luggage, so like persistent unwanted relatives, our bags went wherever we did — which, given the heat and the bags' weight, wasn't far.

Dragging bags, we trudged to a nearby cafe for lunch. Ordered big, with reorders of beer, to extend our stay. As nothing else was nearby, we eventually had to trudge back to the terminal. Metal chairs; no sleeping. Played cards. Read. People-watched. Louise beaded an entire bracelet. A co-ed, teenaged, hormonal Greek scout troop provided entertainment, as did a ballroom dancing club, practicing on the balcony overlooking the (vacant) ferry dock.

At a quarter to nine and no ferry in sight, we inquired about the 9:00 boarding time. "The ferry is late. It will arrive at 1:00 AM. There are too many people between Patras and Venice." Try as we might, we couldn't parse the meaning of that last sentence as it applied to our tardy ferry, but we had five hours to contemplate it (in addition to the nine hours we had already spent there).

The ferry arrived at 1:00 AM Sunday morning. We boarded at 2:00 AM and slept until 11:00 AM Monday. Contrary to our expectations, two days on the luxurious Greek ferry was more like a continuation of the time spent at the terminal: monotonous and lethargic. More reading. More cards. More beads.

Arriving in Venice Tuesday, we wandered in Italian heat for two hours, lost, dragging bags over interminable bridges, trying to find our apartment. It's 6:00 in the evening now. We've napped and we're ready for exploration — just like the good scouts we've become.

Chapter 26: He Said; She Said

In spite of all the efforts of the Greek ferry system, we made it to Venice, the romantic Italian city of Carnival and Casanova. Readers are reminded, however, that it was August, one of the hotter Augusts on record in Italy, and that provoked a certain irritability within our normally amicable duo, resulting in two decidedly antipodal perspectives on the Venetian experience. Here's a post from August 9th, 2013:

$$-\S-$$

Tom says: To my mind, Venice ain't all that it's cracked up to be. It's dirty and stinky and touristy and expensive and crowded and in August, oh-so-hot. Graffiti has embarked on a campaign to cover every vertical surface and all kinds of plastic floats in the canals, vying for dominance with service boats.

Ah yes: the boats. Pictures of Venice invariably show elegant gondolas paddled by happy gondoliers while a loving couple snuggles in the moonlight. In fact, there are no roads in this city. All deliveries (and all garbage) have to be hauled by boat. Buses and taxis and ambulances are boats too, and none of those can be described as elegant. With all that going on, you can forget about the handsome dude in the striped shirt singing *O Sole Mio* while he happily paddles along a quiet Venetian canal. Those few canals that are dedicated to gondolas are crammed with them, cheek to jowl like so many rubber duckies in a washtub. Besides, no one wants to snuggle when it's 95 humid degrees under a hot August sun.

In other words, four days in Venice is enough for me. Louise, on the other hand, is an explorer: she can't leave a place with a clear conscience unless she turns over every rock, and Venice has a lot of rocks. She has been dragging me all over the city until the heat finally overcomes her — it takes about five hours — and only then do I get to rest my aching feet. We've agreed that today we will take canal boats instead of feet, and tomorrow she will explore on her own. Lock up your shoe stores, Venice!

Louise says: Tom and I travel well together, with this one exception. I try to drag him to the most famous tourist attractions so he won't miss anything important. I live in fear that somebody back home will ask: "You were in Barcelona? Didn't you love the Sagrada Familia?" No, we actually never got there. And it would be my fault, wouldn't it?

These expeditions rarely get off the ground before 10:00 AM, involve a long walk to avoid taxi fares or figuring out the bus system, and often land us in the middle of touristville at about noon, the sun high and hot above, the French and Japanese elbowing each other aside.

So it was at St. Mark's Square yesterday, after a dreadfully hot two-hour stroll. "Isn't it glorious?" I kept saying. "Isn't it FABULOUS?" He glanced around at the line outside the basilica and the Doge's palace, watched the orchestra play at the Florian, tried to sit on the steps but got shooed back to his feet by step-monitors, and after about seven minutes total, wanted to leave. He felt the same way about Athens and Istanbul.

I think he feels if it's popular, famous, hot and crowded and expensive, it cannot also be FABULOUS. Feeling grumpy, he started taking pictures of graffiti, rust, peeling paint, rotting wood.

I look around and see beauty everywhere. Palazzi on the Grand Canal, lacy filigree balconies burdened by trailing flowers in pink and peach, roof gardens covered with vines.

Age spots and decay are what one expects of Venice; it's part of what you come to see.

The solution, if there's time, is to take Tom someplace that is not crowded and touristy. Today we got on the city water bus. (We stood on the floating loading dock for awhile, waiting for it to chug away. Duh.) To Tom's bewilderment, I pushed him off at the island of Giudecca, which he'd never heard of. Neither had I, but I knew that the endlessly tasteful Elton John has a house there so it had to be cool.

We let the bus-boat chug away and were stunned by a gorgeous and complete view of the rest of Venice. It's like watching Manhattan from the Brooklyn promenade. We walked down several streets and saw nobody French or Japanese; in fact, we saw nobody at all.

We discovered a huge private estate (not Elton's) that turned out to contain the largest garden in Venice. We bought Cokes at a small shop where they only cost a euro and the owner was happy to see us. We found an empty bench (no monitors) and studied the fabled skyline and watched the many boats come and go.

Tom stayed longer than he had at St. Mark's Square, and he liked it better.

Eventually we got back on the boat bus, landing at San Marco, last stop, on the opposite shore. There, I led him past a jumble of souvenir carts and into the Danieli Hotel lobby. Blissfully air-conditioned, centered by a grand stairway, beamed and painted ceilings, an entire wall made of stained glass, a concierge in a tailcoat and broad tie. This is a historic hotel, a classic along with the Cipriani and the Gritti Palace.

The staff ignored us completely, vermin that we were, while we took pictures. Always ready to patronize a famous bar, I took a peek at the menu. Glasses of wine began at 16 euros, or $21. For 24 euros, ($32) one could have a glass of Veuve Cliquot. That would be the right drink at the Danieli, but we would have to give up lunch (and dinner) to pay for it, and I was growing faint.

Back on the boat, we got off at our San Croce neighborhood and had lunch instead at an Asian-run restaurant that had ninety different kinds of pizza. We skipped over all the horse meat toppings for a simple ham, cheese, and radicchio, and we each drank a liter of water.

Now Tom is napping. Again. I'm tapping my toes. We have a twelve-hour bus-boat pass and there are only seven hours left. Venice is fascinating as long as you stay away from the famous bits. Okay, Tom's right about that. But hey, we're here, let's go!

Chapter 27: These People Carry Weapons

Thankfully (or regrettably: it's a matter of perspective), our days in Venice concluded. Our next apartment was in Italy, on Lake Como, in a town named Bellagio. Two trains and a boat were required. Spanish trains were so civilized; surely Italian trains would be the same.

Perhaps not. Here's my entry dated August 12th, 2013:

— § —

Our journey from Venice to Bellagio was uneventful until we boarded the train from Milan to Como. Reading our Italian tickets as best we could, we determined we had 45 minutes to get from the Milan train to the Como train, in the same station. Couldn't be too hard. But an aggressive porter snatched our bags as soon as the train arrived in Milan and ran off (bags in tow) when we showed him our tickets. There wasn't much for us to do but chase after him.

He sprinted to the Como-bound train and hastily threw our bags aboard. We paid him a seemingly absurd €10 (for ten minutes of work), and joined our bags on the train. As soon as we stepped aboard, the door closed and the train began to move — more than a half hour early!

We had read the tickets wrong of course, misinterpreting our arrival time in Como as our departure time in Milan. Had it not have been for that porter we'd still be standing on the platform, looking for our train. Best ten euros I've ever spent.

We took our seats next to a couple that had stashed their bags — BIG bags — in the aisle next to their seats. More people arrived, dragging their bags behind them. They couldn't get around the bags in the aisle.

In the US, a polite discussion (and probably, an amicable solution) would've ensued. This, however, was Italy. Voices were raised. Fists were shaken. Faces turned red with anger. Louise and I cringed in fear of becoming wounded in what was sure to become an ensuing melee. (The Italian language, lyrical and charming under normal conditions, becomes venomous in anger. We've seen *The Sopranos*: these people carry weapons!)

For us, only twenty minutes remained on the train. We figured we could stand in the aisle for that long, safely removed from the fray. We slunk away as inconspicuously as possible. (Which wasn't very inconspicuous at all: Americans are very tall and very white in Italy.) The scrimmage continued as we watched from a prudent distance, but we saw no bloodshed. Perhaps all that yelling was just the Italian way.

So now we're in Bellagio on the shores of Lake Como, where pretty boats come and go, flowers bloom outrageously, trendy shops and cobblestone streets abound, the sun shines on warm afternoons, and the temperature drops to the low sixties overnight. I visited here on a solo journey in 2001 and vowed to return. Bellagio is that enticing — was then; is now. Our apartment is a tiny studio affair — actually the stable under a converted villa — but it features a large and well-tended garden that's part of the deal. The garden is ours and ours alone, with a private entrance up a cobbled pathway. Within an hour of our arrival, Louise and I began to discuss returning here next summer.

Italy at last.

Chapter 28: Finding an Apartment in a Far-Away Land

We'll stop staring at the garden for a moment while Louise addresses a question that's often asked of us: "How do you find those gorgeous apartments in all those places?" It truly *is* an art. She provided her explanation in a post dated February 28th, 2014:

$-\S-$

Finding apartments to camp in while abroad is the fun job that falls to me. I love it! Who wouldn't love peeking into people's homes in a foreign country? But I have learned much and am ready to pass it on to you, one step at a time:

- Pick some good neighborhoods in your target town. You don't want to live in the middle of a gang war. Exchange email with someone who knows the town, read some travel stories online (I like the *New York Times* travel archive), read good travel magazine websites. Travel blogs can help, too. Most all bigger towns have expat communities; find their websites and ask questions on their forum.
- Make a list of what you ideally want in an apartment, and then cross off "dishwasher," "bathtub," and "clothes dryer."
- Email everybody you know to see if someone knows someone who has a cousin with a chalet in Switzerland, or whatever. Don't feel obliged to take it if it's not what you want.
- Do an early recon of what's out there to get a grip on what is possible on your budget. I always look at websites like AirBnB and HomeAway, but I find better deals in Europe using Venere and HolidayBookings. These sites have multiplied like bunnies since my first search, and are easy to find on Google. There is no one list that has all the available properties.
- After scouting out the prices, pause for a stiff drink and re-adjust your budget. Remember that some rents (in Europe at least) include all utilities, cable TV, and even housekeeping

service. Don't make the mistake of comparing all-inclusive rent like this with the rent you pay on Mulberry Street.

- Look up the property on Google Maps and examine the street view. Dog pound next door? Chalk outline of a body on the sidewalk? Reconsider.

- Read the objective reviews for each property of interest. (Use Trip Advisor, Yelp, or whatever sites apply to your neighborhood.) These will always include a small percentage of cranky customers who just can't stop complaining. Ignore them. Look for clues in the positive reviews, such as "Though the apartment is a six-flight walk up...," or "Despite the scorpions in the shower...."

- Start contacting likely prospects. Flirt a little bit, be charming, explain why you're eager to visit the Auld Sod, claim you're a distant cousin. All this will be helpful in negotiating later on. Ask some questions about the property. If it's important, find out if there is WiFi in the apartment. Sometimes "WiFi available" means at the café two blocks away. If you're going to be there for a month or more, ask if there is a special deal for a longer stay. Often, there is.

- Start a spreadsheet with the nicknames or property numbers of the dwellings down the left column, and across the top note the amenities you value: balcony, view, kitchen, air conditioning, square feet, price range, whatever. It's very, very easy to forget which apartment is which when you get that return note in the mail.

- When the first responses come in, you may come up with nothing but teeny-tiny overpriced apartments. You may go open the window and scream. Or stop looking in France. This is the low-hanging fruit: the more marketing a property does, the more expensive it is.

- Abandon the project, and spend two sleepless nights obsessing. Then go back and look again. Maybe some new places have popped up! Maybe somebody canceled! Check the official city tourist sites or the Chamber of Commerce site. There you will find smaller lodgings whose owners don't bother with the big-web listings. Many foreign cities also have a Craig's List, where you may find a quaint little sublet or vacation house.

- Now some positive answers are coming in. You have chosen a number-one favorite, and your favorite accepts your offer. You write an effusive note of gratitude. Send a deposit via PayPal. Then open a bottle of champagne.

- Keep your communication going with your future hosts, so that they will love you in advance — and not forget you and rent the place to someone else. (Or, as one happened to us, *sell* it to someone else.) Ask more questions, and become their online BFF, without being a pest. They just might meet you at the airport and plant a bottle of wine in your room, as three of our hosts did.

- Even with friendship in the air, expect surprises. One kitchen had such weak stovetop heat that we soaked pasta in warm water instead of boiling it. In Mexico, the Internet only worked outdoors. In one apartment, the upstairs neighbors had about nine children who spent the whole day running back and forth in wooden shoes. Adventure is all about the willingness to be surprised and not fall apart.

- And finally, once you pay your deposit, stop looking. There's no value in renter's remorse. Yes, there will always be a better deal. But you only need the one you have.

Chapter 29: Afloat on a Lake of Envy

With all the various train rides out of the way, we finally arrived in Bellagio. *Bellagio!* I had been waiting to return to Bellagio for twelve years. With our idyllic garden apartment and one of the most beautiful lakeside cities on the planet at our feet, it was easy to make ourselves at home. As an example, here's Louise's post from August 16th, 2013:

−§−

It's easy to get envious around Lake Como, where tony tourists wander around buying diamonds, dining on $25 plates of pasta, and then retire to $900 hotel rooms. Many of these hotels are set in old villas built in the 1800s on the shores of the lake, most of which are still inhabited by the likes of Giorgio Armani and Giorgio Clooney, plus various obscure zillionaires. In an effort to get up close and personal with the enviable lifestyles of the rich and famous, yesterday we took the Midlake Boat Tour. For fifteen euros, we could hop on and hop off at six towns in the area.

First stop was one of the few grand villas where one can wander inside: the 300-year-old *Villa Carlotta*, set on seventeen acres of lush greenery, formal and symmetrical in the Italian style. Inside are grand rooms with sculptures and paintings and highly decorated beamed ceilings, plus a bit of furniture in the bedrooms. The Villa Carlotta was named after Duchess Charlotte of Saxe-Meiningen, when her mother, Princess Marianna of Prussia, gave it to her as a wedding present.

Like many presents from mothers, it was largely ignored. Her new hubby Prince Georg of Saxe-Meiningen had constant business in Berlin, Potsdam, and Meiningen. This fails to explain why, despite separate bedrooms at the Villa, Charlotte bore four children in the five years of her marriage, dying of complications from the last in 1855. She was only 23. It was easy to stop the envy right there.

We moved on to the adjacent town of Tremezzo, dominated by the Grand Hotel Tremezzo, and had lunch at a sidewalk bar. I watched the water while Tom envied the Maseratis, Ferraris, Ducatis, Moto Guzzis, and legions of Fiats.

Well-fed, Tom had a genius idea. We had time to kill as the ferry takes two hours off at lunchtime; we could see the boat anchored far out in the lake, where the crew was probably eating *vitello tonnato* out of Tupperware. Tom suggested we follow the local "Greenway," which in the US is usually a flat trail, once a rail bed, and now a bike trail. This one offered a loop behind the village that would bring us back to the ferry.

We started on a lovely lakeside stroll, watching bathers with rubber shoes mince over the pebble beach to get into the very refreshing (code for very cold) water made of melted snow. The Greenway sign now directed us up a long set of steps. Panting and glowing, I got to the top and saw…another long stretch of steps up. We struggled on, cresting the top only to discover a steep hill path to climb. We made it, stopping often to "admire the view." (Code for pausing, gasping, measuring heart rate, mopping brow.) At this point, the trail turned left and the backpacking German couple ahead of us quit, but we pushed on up one more hill until the path grew flat, and eventually, down.

We reboarded the boat and bypassed the charming village of Varenna. (More about that later, methinks. We were too tired to get off this time.) And finally to the busy town of Menaggio, where several grand hotels monopolized the waterfront with their fancy cafes and swimming pools. (Okay: moment of envy over the swimming pools. Still hot from the hike.)

As we disembarked at our "hometown" of Bellagio, we agreed it was by far the best lakeside town of them all. We wearily slogged our way uphill to our little former-stable (code affordable) apartment, poured two cold vodka tonics, and drank them on our chaises in our garden while boiling up the penne. I had to think of the hot, tired, diamond-encrusted, rich folk milling in the streets below, competing for the last pairs of summer Ferragamos at $400 per pair, and believed at that moment that it is we who are to be envied. It is so simple and calming to be not-rich.

Chapter 30: When Shopping Gets Scary

If there ever was an Olympics of shopping, Louise would take the gold. She certainly trains well for it. After an hour in Best Buy or Home Depot, I'm pretty much ready for a beer. After an entire morning in Nordstrom's Rack, she's just getting warmed up. She can fondle, compare, consider, try on, and haggle endlessly. A pentathlon contestant to be feared.

But the Olympics, as we know, are for amateurs. In spite of her rigorous training regimen, she was no match for the pros in Bellagio. In a post dated August 20th, 2013, she shares her defeat:

— § —

Those of you who know me know that, one or seven times a week, I go out to survey the merchandise in retail stores to see what's new, how it is displayed, and how much it costs. Tom calls this shopping. I call it exploring.

This is usually sheer fun for me, but then I got to Bellagio. It is not Nordstrom's Rack where you paw through the goods, or Ikea, where you drag your own bookcase out of stock, or the Designer Shoe Warehouse, where you dig out your own shoes. That whole self-service thing is not done in Bellagio.

All over are signs that say "Don't try on the shoes! Ask for help! Don't touch anything!" We grubby wanderers must have bruised their fruit, fingerprinted their crystal, broken their china, put snags in their scarves. They must find us tourists barbaric. I don't blame them; it just takes the fun out of it.

In Bellagio, the stores are teeny tiny, but they may have zillions of items in the back room. Thus, when you walk in, there is little to see or touch, but there will be a lady of a certain age who grunts "Buongiorno" just to let you know she is watching to see if you will put your mitts on the merch. "Just looking," I say, floating nonchalantly from rack to rack, counter to counter, conscious of beady eyes upon me. In this kind of store, I slink out the door as quickly and quietly as possible.

In other stores, I am assaulted at the door. "Buongiorno, Signora!" This time the lady of a certain age is all over me. My glance falls upon an elaborate necklace and before I know it, she's putting it on me, reaching high and straining to get to my nape. "Che bella!" She goes on to describe its components, its handmadedness, its rarity, its reasonable price. She steps away. She doesn't take it off and I can't because the clasp is small and behind me. I am forced to wander the store and unable to leave because I'm wearing their necklace.

Then my glance falls upon a different necklace. "Amethyst!" she beams. Before I know it, I'm wearing this one instead. Again, I can't leave. I do not even glance at any more necklaces, but suddenly a third one appears on my neck. By now I am eager to convey that I'm not buying a necklace. While trying desperately to remove the fantasia of mint green beads, I sidestep over the beautiful leather bags and feign interest in a faux Chanel.

She is right there. "Very good quality!" She grabs the bag and shows me the interior pockets and zippers, with a name and function for each. I touch another one. She grabs it. "Very expensive because very good leather! Oh, you like backpack?"

Somehow I convey that I would like the necklace removed, which involves another painful stretch on her part. Fortunately, another shopper comes in and engages my lady. I would like to look at other things in the store but I'm scared to death of disappointing this lovely, hardworking, little woman over and over again. I sneak to the door and then run.

There is a third kind of shop here, so terrifying that I won't even go in. The Missoni store is a good example: a small glass-enclosed jewel, containing only garments in the characteristic Missoni chevron design. In the window is a $240 terrycloth bathrobe with a matching $98 towel. In the store is a single lonely, glum saleswoman, also clad in Missoni chevron. I'm not the only person afraid to go in.

Why am I so uncomfortable? I suppose because I am one of those barbaric touchy-feely tourists who is not going to buy anything. Some people consider Bellagio a shopper's paradise, but they are buying things. It would be a great place to buy things, because the shop folks know their merchandise inside out, and they say things like "With your hair and skin tone, I think this color would be best. Yes!" That frightens me because I would likely fall for it.

Feeling more and more like a fraud, I go to the greengrocer and ask for two tomatoes. That one time I picked up two peaches on my own, I was thoroughly ignored, until Tom saw the sign that said "Not self-service." I know better now.

So, yes, I felt like a clod in stores, so after a week, I stopped shopping and started reading more, beading more, and writing more, which is good. But exploring is a hard habit to break. People ask me if I miss the U.S.A., and I don't, generally. But I just can't wait to get back to Nordstrom's Rack.

Chapter 31: He Lives in Laglio, Which Means Garlic

Fortunately for Louise, there are other diversions in the Lake Como area, namely George Clooney. Below, her post from August 26th, 2013:

$-\S-$

Tom wants nothing to do with this blog entry—an unworthy topic, he feels, a yawn at that. But the readers, especially the girls, have been begging. Can I find him? Did I see him? Is there a new girlfriend? Ever since George Clooney bought Villa Oleandra, the former Heinz mansion, in 2002 for $10 million, his name has been synonymous with Lake Como.

When Lyudmila Putin, the Russian president's wife, visited Como several summers ago, the locals say, the first thing she asked is "Where is the house of George Clooney?" Then she hired a boat to go see it.

All the way up the lake shore that first day, I looked for houses that might be his. Turns out the lake's shores are totally riddled with humongous glamorous villas with 10 or 16 French windows facing the water, so I eventually gave up.

I questioned our landlady, Maria, the first day. "He lives in Laglio, which means garlic," she said. "I've been here nineteen years and have never seen him." The bar next door to us has two glossy black and whites of Clooney on the wall. "He came once, and it was a long time ago," said Henry the waiter.

I had to resort to the trusted source of all legitimate celebrityhood, *Vanity Fair* online. Yes, it turns out the Villa Oleandra is right on the water. Clooney bought it as an investment property but it ended up changing his life, or so he once told a pack of reporters: "I realized how beautiful life was in Italy and how it really helped calm me and not feel so pressured."

(I know just what he means. When I got here, I sat in the chaise in our garden and decided to stay there for three weeks. No need to even get up.)

Villa Oleandra has never been a big secret: it is separated from the road by a fence, a hedge and a video camera, and the pool is visible from the lake. But life is hardly restful. Paparazzi hang out in a garage across the street from George's gate. Several lake boats offer drive-by tours of his villa. Rumor has it that one summer he installed an egg-throwing machine on his dock to pelt vessels that came too close.

But he plays it just right, apparently. He's learning Italian. He's teaching the local kids to play basketball. He bicycles around without bodyguards or even a helmet. His favorite watering hole is Harry's Bar in nearby Cernobbio, where the small Bellinis cost $21, but his picture hangs on the walls of many modest restaurants as well, his arm clutching the owner. Guidebooks and restaurant reviews of the area's eateries almost always include a Clooney endorsement.

So the locals take care of him, sometimes pointing tourists in the wrong direction when they ask the way to George's villa. When he pondered selling in 2010, the mayor begged him to stay. George has since bought properties on either side of Villa Oleandra to use as an editing room and a motorcycle garage. He has built a bridge between them and laced it with ivy so he can cross unnoticed.

Have I seen George? Laglio is maybe an hour and a half away by boat from our apartment. We haven't been there. Also, I don't really care to see George's villa from a boat; I want to see George himself up close. I know it would be possible to launch an aggressive hunt but it would involve expensive boats and bars and the natives would point me the wrong way at every turn. Instead, I just keep in mind that any one the 85 helmeted motorcyclists that go by me every day could be George. Because life is too short to leave this chaise lounge.

Chapter 32: No Place to Live

Like Chania, our stay in Bellagio was only three weeks (a relative measurement, I admit, but after three months in Spain and anticipating six months in Mexico, three weeks didn't seem like much), and again it was time to move on.

Speaking of Mexico, it was time to check in with our contact there. Although we had a month before we were due in Puerto Vallarta, the last time we talked was eleven months prior, and it seemed prudent to say hello.

It may have been better if we just forgot the whole thing. Here's my entry from September 3rd, 2013:

$$-\S-$$

A thousand here, a thousand there — pretty soon you're talking about real money.

(A tip of the hat to the late Senator Everett Dirksen, who, contrary to popular opinion and according to the Dirksen Congressional Center, never said that, or anything like it.)

Back to the thousands: That's the nature of renting apartments around the world. Strike a deal, send a deposit, and hope that no one runs off with the money. We've done that without contracts or other legal instruments ever since we began to travel, and so far we've basked in a glow of mutual trust and respect.

So far.

But Mexico — where we planned to spend six months, where we are headed in just a few weeks, where we hoped to spend enough time to meet some people and learn the language — yes, *that* Mexico...

...well, we have a problem.

We emailed our agent Lupita (I've changed her name because none of this is her fault) a while back: "Are we set?" we asked, our enthusiasm unrestrained. "We'll be there in a few weeks."

There was a pause. A long, email pause.

Finally: "I can't find the owner of the condo!"

That's Lupita, the consummate real-estate professional. Lupita, the unflappable. Lupita, the woman with our money. Lupita, who is now in tears.

The owner is not returning Lupita's calls. Perhaps he has changed his mind. Perhaps he's in another country. Perhaps he's under witness protection. Perhaps he's incarcerated. Maybe he's dead.

Lupita is frantic, but not as frantic as we are. There's a considerable deposit in limbo, six months on the line, and — starting September 28th — no place to live!

Stay tuned.

—§—

So. Life on the road isn't without its perils. We had a few very anxious days to ponder our situation (and sanity: as mentioned above, all of our rental business had been conducted with only a handshake, and a virtual handshake at that), and the pondering was not altogether pleasant.

Fortunately, the pondering was only a few days. Here's my post from September 5, 2013:

—§—

Years ago, a British friend, encountering me after one of life's inevitable missteps, exclaimed, "Tom, you have landed butter-side up!" He meant that I seemed to have recovered well. I've been fond of the expression ever since.

The same can be said of the Puerto Vallarta crisis described in the previous post. Here's the story:

Lupita emailed a day ago. There was a sense of pride in her language. "I have found a villa in the same location for the same price," she said. "Three bedrooms. Photo attached."

A villa? Merriam-Webster defines a *villa* as "a detached or semidetached urban residence with yard and garden space." And the photo that Lupita sent only bent the definition a little: an apartment with a patio overlooking a pool (palm trees, blue agave plants, cerveza in the fridge), and beyond that, the Pacific (sandy beaches, warm saltwater, cerveza on tap).

With three bedrooms and a gourmet kitchen, the villa is a far more luxurious place than the one we had reserved before, but the price is the same. Did Lupita take pity on us and pull a few strings?

Who cares? The villa is grand! Our deposit has been applied to its rent. We've landed butter side up.

$$-\S-$$

Six months in a villa on the coast of Mexico! And three bedrooms! We could have guests!

We heaved a sigh of relief but hardly had time to appreciate our situation, as September found us on the West Coast of the US, visiting friends and family. During that time, I took the opportunity to relieve myself of thirty-one pounds of luggage, including one entire carry-on bag. My other bag — a 36-inch rolling duffel — was so relieved of content that I filled the space with an air mattress — the kind kids use for swimming. It gave the duffel a backbone, which it hadn't had before, and weighed nothing. I just hope the TSA never opens the thing.

Chapter 33: I Left My Heart...

I mentioned our month visiting friends and family on the US West Coast. We have children in Seattle, Portland, and San Francisco; and Louise's brother lives in Calabasas, south of Los Angeles. We have friends, good friends, and we had to see every one.

So our time on the West Coast was a whirlwind of motion. Here's an example, from Louise, dated September 25, 2013:

—§—

I would love San Francisco even if the fabulous firstborn son Ted did not live here. It's always beautiful, always its unique self, and always full of surprises.

The first big surprise this visit was the Walt Disney Family Museum in the Presidio, an army fort that dates back to 1776 and is now a national park. (But a national park with businesses and housing: Google it.)

The new museum chronicles Walt Disney's life via a dazzling march of artifacts, including a model of Disneyland, Mickey Mouse Club clips, and all 32 Oscars (including one "Oscar" with seven mini-Oscars attached, for Snow White). Animation and art are all done up in faultless Disney presentation style. It's such a dense collection that we were tired before we were done.

In between Asian meals, (Ted knows a million such eateries: Chinese, Thai, Vietnamese, Cambodian, Japanese—you name it), we managed to pop over to the de Young Museum to see the new Bulgari jewelry exhibition, sponsored by Maserati. May I just say "Liz Taylor collection"? Now you have the picture.

Sometimes in our most random, unplanned adventures, Tom and I have amazing luck. That happened twice on Monday. First we boarded a streetcar that happened to be San Francisco's very first city-owned car from 1912, appropriately named MUNI 1. It had been retired and revamped and revived and put back to work many times, and was still looking good 101 years later.

MUNI 1 also brought us efficiently to Fisherman's Wharf, where we wandered around the back of Pier 39 only to stumble upon — this is amazing — the final leg of America's Cup race number 16, with the US clearly en route to victory. We could not have had a better view if we had planned and paid for it.

I don't think I've ever had a bad time in San Francisco, but I'm about to leave my heart here once again. On Saturday, it's on to Mexico!

Chapter 34: Used Clothes

We arrived in Puerto Vallarta on September 28th. The villa was everything we had hoped for. Our front yard was a swimming pool. The beach was ten feet beyond that. We were in the tropics, the land of bronze skin and golden sunsets. We used the word "paradise" so often that we pretty much wore it out.

There were flaws, of course. Even the Hope Diamond has flaws. In a post dated October 9th, Louise describes one:

—§—

Sometimes when you go to visit friends in third world countries, you are asked to bring something desperately needed and locally unavailable. Peanut butter. Clinique cosmetics. VooDoo donuts.

But Mexico is better described as a *developing* country, rather than third world. It is sophisticated, wealthy in places, not in financial trouble, and loaded with retail and culture (which to me are pretty much the same thing). Imagine my surprise when I tried to send a box of my own summer clothes down here, only to discover that they had been turned away at the border. (I paid heavily to have them sent back to daughter Sybil.)

It's my fault, of course, for not reading the list of prohibited items provided by our local Mailboxes Etc., a place run by charming Americans and kind of an expat club. I didn't read the list because I thought I knew better, with all the hubris of a frequent flyer. I figured it would only forbid things like firearms, ammunition, plants, fruits, lighter fluid, and ant farms.

Was I wrong! My hot weather duds, some of them actually previously bought in Mexico, come under the heading "used clothes." Hey, those are *my* clothes! It's not like I was getting ready to open a rag market!

So, duly chastened and embarrassed, I read the rest of the list. I was right about the firearms, but I am also forbidden to send myself makeup, medicines, balloons, liquids, stuffed animals, noisy toys, exotic skins, feathers, coins, health and beauty aids, and vitamins. Seriously.

Had I bit the bullet and paid $40 to check an extra bag on the flight down here, I would not have paid about $100 to have my summer clothes shipped to the border and then back to Portland again, with the result being that I still do not have them. (Apparently, carrying your stuff into Mexico is not the same as "importing" it.) So let that be a lesson to me. The only way I could throw more money at this issue would be to fly back and get the clothes myself.

The point is, when you come to visit us, do not bring peanut butter. Talk to Sybil and bring some of my clothes.

Chapter 35: Opportunities for Wonder

The blog presented lots of challenges, but its rewards far exceeded any fuss. Perhaps the greatest reward was one of observation: knowing that we were going to write about a place or a moment sharpened our senses and magnified our memories. We saw things through our readers' eyes and often those things provoked wonder.

We were in Mexico for six months. There were plenty of opportunities for wonder. Below, some examples:

$$-\S-$$

(Louise, writing December 16th, 2013.) The other day I was watching Portlandia in the afternoon down here in Mexico. It was that episode about the annual day in July when the first beam of sunshine returns to Portland after eight months of gray and drizzle. People come rushing out doors with their picnics, bongo drums, sun hats, skateboards, and guitars. I instantly doubled over with guilt, verklempt with shame, suffering a double dose of Sun Guilt in both art and life. The sun was shining, and I was inside making a bracelet. I should have been Out There.

You see, I grew up on the East Coast, where every week of the year included both sunny days and wet days. On the sunny days we went out to play, on the rainy ones we Got Things Done. It all worked out. I contracted Sun Guilt when I moved to Oregon seven years ago. When the weather was gray and rainy for eight months in a row, I Got Stuff Done, including the lecture series I gave on Seasonal Affective Disorder, and still had time to go to daytime movies, bead in front of the television, make clothes, and enjoy Happy Hours in bars with roaring fireplaces.

But then summer comes, and the sun shines in Portland, inexorably, even monotonously, every day from July 4 to October 10. That first summer, I kept waiting for a rainy day so I could Get Something Done. Nada. Nul. Zip. Zilch. "Oh," one the natives told me. "Nobody works in the summer here." Here is the Sun Guilt droning monologue: Move it, sister. Step away from the computer/kitchen/

television/sewing machine/craft table/treadmill and get out there. The sun will not last forever!

But it is sunny in Puerto Vallarta almost every day, at least during the half year that we're here. I'm not good at doing nothing, so afraid of being bored stiff, I plotted a novel to be written, bought a sewing machine to play with, and enlarged my bead stash to make new treasures. Those are all my favorite things, but they are indoor sports. I feel I can't do anything right. I do my walk, swim, and get my brief doses of Vitamin D sitting outdoors in the sun with a book. All during that time I feel guilty about not being inside making things. When I go inside and make things, I get the big slap of Sun Guilt. Somehow, I don't do a lot of either baking or making. People complain about SAD. When will there be a cure for the little-discussed SG?

But it's not that bad. You know what's really bad? Sun*set* Guilt! Sunset Guilt happens around 6 p.m. when the sun is getting bigger and brighter and about to slide down into a pile of clouds that will instantly turn hot pink, in a different pattern every night, and Tom and I are on a bus or in some restaurant downtown and not on our patio at the edge of the sea watching every second of that sunset's festive glory.

And so, more often than not, we pour margaritas and settle in our lounge chairs facing west over the Pacific, and the show goes on for an hour, and we just can't be anywhere else. Like the sun, that view is not going to be ours forever. Only six months. Now and then we may say, "We should go out to eat/sightsee/visit!" But we stay put. Sun Guilt is one thing, but Sunset Guilt is just too much to bear.

(Louise, writing October 28, 2013) We live right on the beach, so when we go downtown or uptown, we take the blue bus. For 45 American cents, we can go just about anywhere we need to.

You know which bus to take because the stops are painted on the front window. What a genius idea to have the stops on the outside of the bus instead of the inside! No vague street names either; the destinations are clearly and concisely the names of the stops: Walmart, or Aeropuerto, or Sam's Club. The bus roars and rattles up to your stop, opening its door before it comes to a halt. The tires are gigantic, so you take a big step off the curb and climb a steep stairway to get to the driver, who takes your money (no passes; no transfers; cash only) and hands you a damp, limp ticket made of newsprint, which nobody ever checks.

Outside the window we see glamorous resorts, tumbledown hovels, taco carts, and local businesses that sell funeral flowers, flooring, Asian foodstuffs, shoes, and shiny fabrics. It goes past the big soccer field where some coach is always torturing a team of little uniformed players in the heavy heat.

Inside, each bus is individually decorated by its driver. There'll be a ragged front curtain for a sun visor, maybe a grimy stuffed bear lashed to the dashboard, and perhaps a religious icon, most often Our Lady of Guadeloupe, Jalisco state's preferred virgin.

My favorite of these is a Photoshopped picture of Bus U-066, with Jesus behind it, inscribed with the Driver's Prayer. The driver asks for patience and safety from fire and accident, to be safe from the temptation to speed, to carry everyone safely to his or her destination, and even calls upon San Cristobal, the transportation saint, at the very end. I'd ride that bus anytime.

The rest of the interior of any blue bus is usually a disaster. Filmy, cracked windows that may or may not open, hard plastic seats that are faded, possibly split, and often tagged with spray paint. An old linoleum floor that is lifting at the corners. Hot sunshine pounds on the sun-side passengers; when people leave a shady seat, somebody will slide over from the sunny side and nab it. If you're lucky, you might get a warm wind in your face, or get to put your elbow out the window.

Mimes, guitar players, singers, and even stand-up comedians sometimes board the bus and perform for tips. The bad ones are tolerated; the good ones are applauded; they're all tipped.

And what a ride! There aren't enough words like "lurch" and "jolt" to describe it. The bus roars, screeches to brake, starts suddenly, throws standees into people's laps, barrels ahead and teases other buses by passing with one inch of breathing space. It would be fruitless to fix the suspension. The cobblestones are so destructive that it just wouldn't last. You just gotta let it rattle.

Your fellow travelers are mothers with babies, hotel workers in uniform, cute schoolkids in uniform, people going to work, jaded expats, and in high season, a sprinkling of brave tourists. The natives help you find your way, and everybody is just tolerating the jouncing and the heat.

Here's the best part: your blue bus is supposed to arrive every ten minutes or so. In fact, they arrive much more often. Sometimes they're stacked up at the stop, waiting for you. Of course, if you can't handle that level of service, there are alternatives.

You could take one of the zillion cabs, and they too are cruising for you. But that would cost you five dollars. The blue bus is one tenth of that. And there's no charge for prayers, cute kids in uniforms, or on-board entertainment.

(One more from Louise, dated January 4th, 2014) As I sit here I am surrounded by happy Mexican extended families and their kids and dogs. Los Tules is crowded because of the holidays. And though these are well-bred, peaceful folks by day, they don't seem to have a fixed bedtime, and neither do their children. The party rages on, late into the night.

Mexicans, we have decided, love to party. It is one of their most endearing traits. And as an excuse to party, they have a wickedly long holiday season. We are only halfway through.

First there was the Day of the Dead on November 2. The Aztecs celebrated this 3000 years ago for the entire month of August. The Catholic Spaniards shifted it to All Saints day, thus shortening the party, but the Mexicans had their revenge by barely pausing to breathe.

Two weeks later it was Revolution Day, when a ginormous parade wended its way through downtown Vallarta. Most impressive were the policemen who did motorcycle tricks, standing on their seats, piling up other cops into a pyramid atop two bikes, and an infinite variety of gymnastics on wheels. (To our scaredy cat American friends: doesn't this prove how little crime there is in Puerto Vallarta? That the police have time to perfect this?)

The parade included dancing horses, fife and drum corps, school bands, dance teams, and fire trucks, and went on all day and night. And then there's a party.

But wait! There's more! Another two weeks to breathe and redecorate, and then then begins the ten-day festival of our Lady of Guadeloupe. She is Spanish, not Mexican, but she has been wholly adopted as a secular heroine throughout the country. This means that even Jewish Mexicans have her statue around. She's just like everybody's mother.

The festival involves a week and a half of daily processions, each with different local participants, through streets lined with pop-up Mexican treat stands. And then there's a party.

Three days after that, the posada season begins. This commemorates the pre-natal excursion of Mary and Joseph, looking for a place to give birth, visiting one inn after another along the way. The modern version involves bringing a potluck dish to somebody's house. The host cleans and makes the house ready, but doesn't cook. It is also the name given to the office Christmas parties at long tables in good restaurants, which are nevertheless just as awkward as ours. Still, there's a party every night.

Skipping over the Solstice parties for now, we proceed to Christmas Eve, when gifts are exchanged and midnight Mass is enjoyed. We weren't here for Christmas this year, but I remember a lonely Mexican Christmas Eve when I was sitting by a desperately flu-ish Tom. The children from the neighboring room in the hotel knocked on our door with little wrapped presents in hand. Our hearts got all warmed up. Then, there was a party.

December 28 was The Day of the Holy Innocents, commemorating Herod's murder of baby boys. For some reason, this is celebrated as Mexico's April Fool's Day. That must be why somebody set off a series of very loud fireworks outside the villa the other morning at 2:30.

It's only a couple of days to The Day of the Holy Kings on January 6, when Mexican children get another windfall of presents, this time from the latecomers to the stable. I understand the snack shacks and processions will be back. I sure hope there's a party.

Chapter 36: Full-Time Travel is a Bargain

In response to hearing about our vagabond lifestyle, people often say, "I'm so envious!," or "You are so brave!," but the question we probably get the most is "How can you afford to live like that?"

We don't have responses for the first two comments, but the money matter is an easy one. Here's my post from February 7, 2014:

$-\S-$

I've never stopped to think about it, but now that I do, I find it surprising that for people who travel as much as we do, we hardly ever talk about money. We didn't meet each other until we were in our sixties, so we each brought our own finances to the relationship. As time went on we never merged our finances, electing instead to establish a joint bank account to which we contributed whenever it got low. The joint account pays for rent, food, and other common expenses. Other than that, we each have our own checking and investment accounts to do with as we please. The other night, during our customary cocktail at sunset, we just happened to mention our individual savings accounts: They have grown considerably since we began our travels.

We added up our expenses for the past ten months and indeed, it has cost us less—far less—to live than it did while we lived in Portland. In other words, for us full-time travel has been a money-saving venture. And an adventure to boot. How can that be?

Here's a listing of things we do NOT pay for:

- Mortgage
- Home maintenance and repairs (or HOA dues)
- Property taxes
- Homeowner's insurance
- Electricity, gas, sewer, water
- Internet access
- Cable TV

And just the other day I read a gem from a fellow expat concerning state income tax. Since expats can declare residence in any state we choose, he chose a state with no income tax. There are plenty of mail forwarding services that fill that need.

Everything on that list above was covered in the rent we paid. The most we paid was $1800 per month (Bellagio), but it—like the rent we paid in Greece and Mexico—included housecleaning and laundry service.

Oh yes: we don't have a car. Buses, taxis, and trains get us where we want to go, at an average cost of about $60 a month—a little more in Greece; much less in Mexico. No payments, no repairs, no fuel, no insurance, no parking—cars are *expensive!*

People often say, "How can you afford your lifestyle?" To which we respond, "How do you afford *yours?*"

Chapter 37: Trouble in Paradise

Life in Paradise continued to beguile us. Mexican food was all around us, and all of it was divine. As something called the "Polar Vortex" paralyzed half the United States, we reclined by the pool slathered in SPF 50. The surf continued to susurrate outside our bedroom window. And the Mexican people continued to charm us with their sense of humor, family values, and trust.

On the other hand, nothing—not even Paradise—is perfect. Here are some entries describing the darker side of our haven, beginning with one of my own from December 29th, 2013:

—§—

It's Christmas Week in Mexico. For many it's a week off, and in Mexico where the family is cardinal and most people live inland, Christmas Week is spent at the beach. Los Tules has beaches (a half mile of them) and swimming pools (seven). This is the place for Mexicans to take their families for Christmas Week, and scores of Mexicans have done just that.

There's just one hitch: it's raining.

Puerto Vallarta (which is where Los Tules is located) is in the tropics, where there are two seasons: wet (May through October) and dry (November through March). Thus it's supposed to be dry here now. People pack up the family and travel hundreds of miles to be here during the dry season, and this year they got here just as the rain arrived. It's like National Lampoon's "Vacation": Wally World is closed.

Rain is here and it's predicted well into next week.

Here in Puerto Vallarta, people wear sandals. Until I visited Portland for Christmas, I hadn't worn shoes in six months. But when it rains, sandaled feet are soggy feet, especially in the city where cobblestone streets puddle with fallen rain. People congregate in the city when the pool and the beach are out of commission, but they're no happier there than they were at the beach. In other words, when it rains during Christmas Week, it's best to stay inside.

Don't tell anyone, but Louise and I are pleased. We're here for six months; a week of rain is welcome. The pool is just outside our front door. The rain keeps the mob out of the pool. When the mob is out of the pool, it's quiet. The rain also grants us license to stay inside. I watch sports on TV. Louise crafts with her new bead loom. We both nap. This morning we slept in, well past sunrise. I'm sorry about Wally World, but the quiet and the down time are priceless. Hedonism has never had a better advocate.

(Tom, a post from November 5, 2013)

4:30 PM I take a bottle of water from the refrigerator. It begins to drip before I get it to the patio, instantly sheathed in condensation as if it had been dipped in wax. It is eighty-eight degrees and the humidity is more than that. A storm is coming to Puerto Vallarta.

In the kitchen, Louise is preparing paella, boiling water for rice, frying things in a pan. She has the air conditioner on. Without it, she would wither in the kitchen like a stick of melted butter. We try not to use the air conditioner, preferring to acclimate to the tropical weather. But in the kitchen with a hot stove, acclimating is no more practical than breathing fire.

5:15 PM I prepare our drinks: a Margarita for me, a Cape Codder for her. The glasses instantly sweat in the humid air. We take them to the beach, recline under a palapa. Severo, the basket vendor, comes by. Louise bought a basket from him yesterday ("My family make them here in Puerto Vallarta") but she didn't have enough cash to pay for it in full. Severo gave her the basket anyway and said he'd catch up with her later for the remainder. We talk for half an hour. Laugh a lot. The people here are like that: industrious, friendly, trusting, cheerful.

6:00 PM It is time for another spectacular Puerto Vallarta sunset. We sit on the beach with our drinks nearly every night to watch the sunset, but tonight — given the density of the sky — it is not to be. The sky and the sea, both as gray and dense as used motor oil, confuse the horizon. Rather than a sunset, we go simply from light to dark in that unfamiliar way of the tropics, as suddenly as if we blew a fuse.

6:15 PM Lightning, out at sea. I count the seconds, awaiting thunder. In air, sound travels about a mile every five seconds. It is eighteen seconds before we hear thunder. The storm is about three miles away.

6:30 PM It's the Fourth of July out there, with lightning striking as often as fireworks. Thunder rumbles like severe indigestion. I count five seconds now. The storm is near, and drawing nearer. Quickly.

6:45 PM Lightning and thunder surround us. We are living inside a Leyden jar. Until a moment ago, the air — enveloping us like a warm blanket — was as still as a corpse. Suddenly the wind has picked up, whipping rain under the palapa. Palapas' roofs are made of tightly woven palm fronds and they're remarkably waterproof. We've been sitting beneath ours, ogling the storm, wide-eyed, whispering "Wow!" and "Lookitthat!" like children at a circus. But palapas have no walls and now the wind has found us, and brought along its friend the rain. The rain has an attitude. We grab our glasses and sprint for home.

Our patio is less than a hundred feet from the palapa but by the time we're under cover we might as well have been swimming. My hair and my clothes are soaked but I don't care: the rain is as warm (and welcome) as a mother's hug.

7:00 PM The wind, the thunder and the lightning stop abruptly, but the rain is here for an extended engagement. Louise serves paella on the patio. We light a candle, pour a bottle of wine, and eat while the rain cascades in sheets off the patio roof.

It has been dry in Puerto Vallarta. People are worried about having enough water to last the winter. After tonight, perhaps, not so much.

(One more, again from me, dated December 9, 2013)

Everyone who knows Louise knows that she's a varsity-level shopper. Leaving the theater last night, she lingered at numerous shop windows even though the shops were closed. Closed! When the shops are closed, she plans strategy. When they're open, she manipulates prices, selections, and even vendors with the precision of an NBA star on a charge to the basket. The woman is shopping's Kobe Bryant.

Thus you can imagine her enthusiasm for the annual opening of the Old Town Farmers' market in Puerto Vallarta's Emiliano Zapata district, a district where gringos gather to worship the gods of Mexican cuisine, art, and apparel.

Now before you form a romantic image of a quaint Mexican outdoor market in a charming colonial village, note that the first vendor we encountered was a Portlander. His wife attended Le Cordon Bleu College there. Louise bought buckets of his pesto, which immediately leaked into my backpack. Another Americano, in the business of growing peanuts and making peanut butter for PV's peanut-butter-starved gringo market ("I quit my day job last year,") caught my eye. In fact, most of the market's booths were staffed by gringos.

There were handmade clothes, sexy firefighter calendars (which I had autographed as a present for my daughter), silver jewelry, hand-rolled cigars, and preservative-free dog food. The (human) food and the music were typical Puerto Vallarta, which is to say exquisite. It was all very festive and sunny; this is the best time of the year in PV.

We've visited markets in five countries now. Interestingly, they all included zapatos (shoes — Louise's favorite) except one, and that one was in the Emiliano Zapata District of PV. You'd think, with a name like Zapata, the district's market would feature zapatos, but no: no zapatos. But really now, do NBA fans riot when Kobe misses a layup? No. Do Zapatistas (the shoppers, not the revolutionaries) riot when there are no shoes at the PV market? Of course not, not when there are so many other options. Besides, Sybil got a hunky firefighter and I got chunky peanut better. Who needs shoes?

Chapter 38: Going Home

In spite of living in Paradise, in spite of the monetary savings, in spite of the adventure and the discovery, by February we had made a decision: we would return to Portland. Here's my entry from February 5th, 2014:

—§—

Traveling as we do, we meet a lot of people. Conversations ensue. Questions are asked, and among the first is, "Where do you live?" Then the familiar words: *vagabond, expat, ne'er-do-well,* and *homeless.*

Homeless.

After we tell the story of our travels—so well-rehearsed we can recite it in our sleep—comes the inevitable question: "What will you do next?"

Our answer has always been, "We don't know." But now, with less than sixty days remaining of our planned expat adventure—less than sixty days!—we have decided.

We're going home.

Note how I gave "homeless" its own paragraph up there. It turns out that homelessness is the bane of the expat adventure. Nothing, we have learned, makes one appreciate home more than being...

...homeless.

Relax. I'm not going to subject you to a bromidic treatise on the romance of having a home. As a guy I'm obliged to identify the empirical and pragmatic, to illuminate the practical; to list, dispassionately, the logic that has brought us to our decision.

In no particular order, these are the things we miss in our travels:

Friends and family. Bless the hearts of those who have traveled to visit us in faraway places, but the very fact that we're far away most of the time gnaws at us like heartbreak. We long for one of those conversations that begins, "Whacha doin' tonight," and being able to follow up on it. When I said "In no particular order," this is the exception. Above all, we miss our people!

Reliable Internet. Like running water, we take the Internet for granted until it's gone. Email, Netflix, Pandora, Amazon, maps and search—try it: live for a week without the Internet. We haven't enjoyed good service since Spain. Seven months!

Phone service and texting. Our children prefer texting over all other forms of distant communication. We used phones to reconnect when we were separated in a mall, or in a city, or even in the same neighborhood. We used phones to transact business. Sometimes we even used them for pleasant conversations. But no more. We have phones and we have phone numbers but we are flummoxed when it comes to their use. All assistance is in a foreign language and our hands are thrown up in despair.

Quality sound reproduction. This is my thing. Louise isn't particularly interested. But have you ever listened to Schubert or watched *Terminator 5* through the tiny speakers on a TV set? Give me woofers and tweeters and everything in between!

A permanent mailing address and phone number. Go ahead, try completing an insurance claim, a visa application, an order from Amazon without them. Try it. I rest my case.

Our own pots, pans, and knives. Years have gone into our collection of pots and pans (which we still have, in storage), and we haven't used a sharp knife since we packed up our kitchen in Portland.

A washer and dryer. We had a washer in Spain, but that was seven months ago. We've been washing our stuff in the sink ever since. And a dryer! In Spain the clothesline was five stories above another apartment's roof. Socks especially (always one, never a pair) committed suicide from that clothesline every day, it seemed, leaving their carcasses sixty feet below where we could mourn them in futility. In Greece we dried clothes on the balcony. In Italy, in the garden. And in Mexico we really don't dry them at all, given the humidity of the tropics.

A familiar grocery store, a bank, a hardware store. I yearn for peanut butter, maple syrup, good beer, and an inexpensive set of screwdrivers.

Stuff. Yeah, we know: we sold all our stuff and bragged about it. But Louise would like a hair dryer, and we would like some colorful bowls for our cereal. I would like that set of screwdrivers. But we're on the road: If it has to be packed, it's not gonna happen.

The list goes on.

So. What's next? We've rented a furnished apartment in Portland for the month of April. During that time we're going to search for a condo to buy or a long-term apartment to rent there. We'll settle in and hang our own stuff on the walls. We'll dry our clothes with a machine. I'll tighten that loose faucet with my own screwdriver.

Will we travel again? Of course we will! I want to pilot a canal boat in France. We want to visit Ireland. And we plan to return to Puerto Vallarta next winter. This is not the end of adventure. It's the end of *an* adventure, and it's the beginning of a new one.

Chapter 39: In Mexico, It Was Time for Another Margarita

You will recall my medical event almost a year ago in Spain. Chapters 16 through 19 addressed the event. Medical insurance was mentioned, but a financial resolution was not. I paid twenty thousand dollars to a Spanish hospital; was I ever reimbursed? The answer was not to be found in this book until now.

Disclaimer: If you read this book as a travelog, I will forgive you if you skip this chapter. There's no new territory to explore here. On the other hand, some of you are interested in the practical elements of full-time travel: finance, transportation, preparation, and insurance. To paraphrase Anheuser-Busch, this chapter is for you. This is a log of my traveler's medical-insurance events, from inception to resolution. May they rest in peace.

Another disclaimer: My insurance policy is a MediCare supplement. It is not an insurance rider of some sort, nor is it travelers' medical insurance. Long ago, when I applied for travelers' medical insurance and listed all of my pre-existing conditions (three heart attacks, numerous strokes, chronic hypertension), I could almost hear them snicker at the other end of the email. My application was politely declined.

All right. With all the disclaimers out of the way, here's my post from March 28, 2014:

—§—

April 22, 2013: In Spain, a sudden severe headache sends me in search of medical care. I am hospitalized and require brain surgery.

Medications from the brain surgery provoke a heart attack a week later. There is more surgery, but I'm cleared for release in early May. The hospital bill is $20,000 US, which I pay personally.

June 4, 2013: I submit a $20,000 claim to my insurance carrier using their online claim form, requesting a wire transfer of the cash to my bank account. The wire transfer option is the first option listed on the form.

June 18, 2013: I submit another claim form for $497.88, to cover four follow-up appointments at the hospital.

August 21, 2013: I email my insurance carrier asking if there has been any progress on my two claims. They respond by saying that yes, they did receive the claim, but "due to the fact that the direction of pay was a wire transfer, the claim was stalled." (You'll recall that a wire transfer was the first payment option available on the claim form.) They also say that, "A further review of our records indicate that we have received returned mail. On June 18, 2013, we attempted to call you at [my discontinued US phone number], which is no longer in service." This delay, to my mind, was reasonable. The only one.

My initial email was sent via my personal email account. All the rest of our communication transpired via a secure email network that was operated by the carrier.

August 22, 2013: I write back, explaining that we don't have a permanent address or phone number, that we're vagabonds, living a life on the road. This may have been an error.

August 22, 2013: The insurance carrier responds by saying, "At this time we are looking into the demographic changes given."

August 27, 2013: Another note from the carrier: "Please note that your permanent address must be inside our service area in order for you to be a member of [my insurance plan]. You may request that we send mail to you at another address outside our service area. You may also temporarily reside for up to 12 months outside our service area and remain a member...." They also indicate that they had sent a "residence verification letter" to my daughter's address in Portland, which is the address I have been using for paper mail. The residence verification letter must be hand-signed.

August 30, 2013: A $432.54 check to cover the June 18th claim arrives. My daughter deposits it into my account. No mention is made of the June 4th $20,000 claim.

September 11, 2013: Louise and I have returned to the US for the month of September. I collect the residence verification letter from my daughter, sign it, and send it back to the carrier.

September 13, 2013: An email from the carrier says, "The international claim...has [been] processed and payment has been sent to you...." *Hallelujah!* The check is in the mail!

September 25, 2013: No check has been received. I inquire politely.

September 30, 2013: The carrier emails to remind me that a check was mailed August 30th, 2013 and cashed. Well, that's true. See above. *A* check. Not *the* check.

October 1, 2013: I respond to the email above by saying, "I submitted a much larger claim (in the neighborhood of $20,000). That's the one I am inquiring about. Any news on that one?"

October 2, 2013: Their reply, "Our records do not indicate a second claim.... We are researching this issue...."

October 4, 2013: The carrier asks me to resubmit the June 4th claim. Miraculously, although I am now living in Mexico and three prior countries of residence have passed, I still have the original claim in my suitcase and am able to copy the form and comply with their request (see below).

October 7, 2013: I email an electronic copy of the original claim form and receive a thank-you note from the carrier a few hours later. The note also contained my favorite line from all of our correspondence: "It is possible they missed the facility bill...." ("They," in this context, being another department of the carrier's office.) In other words, the carrier is saying that they have been completely ignorant of my $20,000 claim since its inception, in spite of their statement August 21 saying that they had received it.

It's interesting to note that this email was deleted from their system soon thereafter. None of the other emails were. Fortunately, I made a copy for my records before it disappeared.

January 9, 2014: Three months pass. I email the carrier again, asking if there has been any progress.

January 10, 2014: The carrier replies saying that they have sent mail to my Spanish hospital asking for copies of all my records and that the hospital hasn't responded. Their email concludes by saying, "The claim has been denied at this time due to 'requested information not received.'" In Mexico, it was time for a margarita.

January 13, 2014: I email the hospital myself, requesting my records.

January 14, 2014: The hospital emails back within 24 hours, saying the records have been sent to my daughter's address. Quite fortunately, my daughter was scheduled to visit us in Puerto Vallarta soon thereafter, and when she does she brings the records with her.

January 28, 2014: I scan nineteen pages of hospital records and email everything to the carrier.

February 25, 2014: An email from the carrier: "We have completed processing of claim [number redacted] for date of service April 22, 2013. A reimbursement check will be sent to you...." I email my daughter, telling her to be on the lookout for the money. In Mexico, it was time for another margarita.

March 5, 2014: An email from my daughter in Portland says: "The check has arrived." She photographs the check and all the accompanying paperwork, attaches the photos to an email and sends it to me. The check is for $10,649, $9,750 short of the $20,399 I paid the hospital. Almost all of the unpaid claim is for hospital room charges.

Naturally, I'm perturbed. I ask a friend—he has been in the insurance business for almost fifty years—to look everything over. He explains that the overseas section of my policy promises to cover "emergency medical costs," and that most of the room charges were not emergency in nature. To paraphrase my friend: "Nine thousand dollars to have people save your life—twice—seems like a bargain to me." He's right, as he usually is. That's why I called on him to help.

March 21, 2014: I ask my daughter to deposit the check and the matter is closed. Total time required from my original claim submission until payment: nine months.

Regardless of the nature of one's coverage—Medicare supplement, travelers' rider, or travelers' medical—anyone embarking on an expat adventure such as ours had best have either a ready line of credit or plenty of money in the bank. Hospitals in far-away countries do not like to collect from American insurance companies (I can't imagine why), and some hospitals, like mine, will not release you until you've paid in full.

To be specific: Have money in the bank, be monastically patient, and be prepared to ask how high when they tell you to jump.

In Chapter 38, I listed some of the things we miss the most by not having a permanent home. I omitted one important item: **a nearby in-network medical facility**. Having brain surgery and a heart attack was bad enough; the added insult of pursuing a lengthy and expensive insurance claim was simply tyrannical.

Adventure is a wondrous thing. Most of it.

Chapter 40: I'm So Glad We Did This

Our days in Mexico (and indeed, as expats) were drawing to a close. Each of us wrote a final entry before we boarded the plane to the US. Here is Louise's, dated March 31, 2014:

—§—

What have I learned in a year away from home? Here are the top ten things:

1) Life can change drastically in a heartbeat. I guess I knew that, but I'd never watched someone so close to me so suddenly close to death. Tom's episode was a life-changer.

2) It is possible to live without a home address and phone service, but it's *really hard*.

3) Wherever we went, we saw multi-generational families together every Sunday, brunching and strolling in tribes everywhere. With my kids so far away, I was in tears on Thanksgiving, and a recovering motherholic all through December. I'm okay now. Especially with this new plan to pester them incessantly from now on. Maybe invite them over every weekend. Be the mother-in-law from hell.

4) Mexicans are really, truly, lovely people.

5) Wearing sandals for a whole year is even better than you think.

6) Our theory that Europeans seem, culturally, more generous and familiar with strangers truly held up. And we needed that a lot when Tom was ill. Our friends in Spain did all they could to translate medical Catalan, keep Tom entertained, keep me sane, and celebrate his birthday right after the hospital. I come home with more emotional and hospitable generosity.

7) I really missed the old friends who know our stories. The people you don't have to keep introducing yourself to. The people you can trust. The people who invite themselves to our Oscar party. I missed our Oscar party.

8) I don't need a lot of stuff. I don't even need a lot of clothes. I hope that statement does not come back to haunt me.

9) One of our many miracles was that Tom and I spent a year pretty much alone together without brickbats or even boredom. But it made me treasure my girlfriends now more than ever. I miss the girlfriends who tell you to go ahead and spend the money. And you look like you've lost weight. And let's go to a movie in which there is Pierce Brosnan and also nothing explodes.

10) It is possible to live by the sea for six months in a row, hearing it roll and roar 24/7, and never once take it for granted. Who cares if there was no phone service or movies on demand? I am one of the luckiest people on earth. And I will always treasure the memories this year.

In a little over forty-eight hours we will begin a new chapter in life, as we return to Portland to search for a new apartment. I am sad. I am happy. But above all I am so glad we did this.

Chapter 41: Use Your Feeling Words

My final post, uploaded three hours before our plane lifted off April 2, 2014, appears below:

— § —

The therapist's mantra: "How do you feel about…"

Lord help me. I'm a guy. We talk about horsepower and RBIs; we don't talk about *feelings*. How do I *feel* about leaving the expat lifestyle? How do I *feel* about moving back to Portland? How do I *feel* about having a home again?

Could I just have a list of feeling words and I'll pick a few?

But no, the therapist wants me to find my own feeling words. I imagine Doctor Melfi, crossing those long legs and leveling that infinitely patient, frustratingly silent, expressionless stare into my eyes, waiting for my reply: How do I *feel* about …

Okay. Here it comes. Wait for it…

I. Feel. *Homesick.*

I was homesick once before. I was twelve or thirteen, scheduled for an overnight stay at an out-of-town friend's house. It was the my-dog-just-got-run-over-by-a-car type of homesick. There were projectile tears. I didn't even last until dinnertime. Mom had to come get me.

This is not a car-hits-dog type of homesick. Mom doesn't need to come get me. I'm not sad or lonely or desperate. Can I define it with words? The definition is as elusive as the definition of love. When we talk of love we depend on the listener's empathy to complete the gestalt. You can't define love with a recitation of its component parts.

The same goes for homesickness. I can talk about comfort, familiarity, and control. I can talk about a lasting community and a common language. I can talk about a permanent address and phone number. I can talk about my own pictures on the walls, my favorite foods in the fridge, my pillowy comforter on the bed. But I can't assemble all those parts into a description of home, or, in its absence, this homesick feeling.

In Chapter 6 I suggest that "home is where the head is." Louise and I haven't used the word "home" to describe the place we're living for almost a year. In spite of the wonderful people in Spain, in spite of Greece's luscious beaches, in spite of the serenity of Bellagio, we never thought of any of them as home. And here in Puerto Vallarta, in spite of having spent almost six months in one apartment, we don't think of it as home either. If home is where the head is, we haven't been home for almost a year. No wonder I'm homesick.

So now I'm about to return to Portland to look for the cure. Like an audience before the curtain rises, I'm impatient and anticipant. I'm feeling homesick, yes, but I'm also feeling hopeful; I'm feeling sanguine; I'm enthusiastic and eager and intoxicated by the potential of going home again.

We depart at 3:00 this afternoon. Let the curtain rise.

~~~~

P.S. for Doctor Melfi: I used eight feeling words in the penultimate paragraph. Can I watch NASCAR now?

Chapter 42: Is It Over?

We flew to Portland that day. Ten days later we signed a long-term lease on an apartment downtown.

Starved for companionship, we booked friends and relatives almost back-to-back. When we weren't socializing, we hounded IKEA for furniture, filed change-of-address forms (an address of our own!), and secured real phone numbers for the first time in a year. Our children texted. Our friends called. We were citizens of the universe once again.

Is it over? It's never over. Like love, adventure is too precious an opportunity to neglect.

We have unpacked our bags...

...but not our passions.

Made in the USA
Lexington, KY
09 November 2017